LUCIFERIAN SPIRIT AMONG THE PROPHETS

I0519014

Ken Cox

REJOICE
Essential Publishing

Copyright © 2024 by Ken Cox

All rights reserved. No part of this publication may be reproduced, distributed or transmitted in any form or by any means, including photocopying, recording, or other electronic or mechanical methods, without the prior written permission of the publisher, except in the case of brief quotations embodied in critical reviews and certain other noncommercial uses permitted by copyright law. For mission requests, write to the publisher, addressed " Attention: Permissions Coordinator," at the address below.

Ken Cox/Rejoice Essential Publishing
PO BOX 512
Effingham, SC 29541
www.republishing.org

Luciferian Spirit Among The Prophets/Ken Cox

ISBN-13: 978-1-956775-87-7

FOREWORD

As is his custom, Apostle Cox writes with the passion he believes is necessary to inform the Body of Christ. He wants the reader to understand this spirit and how it operates not only in the Body of Christ, but specifically in the prophetic.

He lays this spirit out pretty much line by line and precept by precept. The reader should understand who, what, why, how, and when of this spirit and how it operates. Not only that, but he also explains how to identify this spirit.

In our walk with God, we are aware of spiritual warfare. We have had classes and read books concerning the different spirits in operation, what they look like and how we are to overcome them. This spirit has been overlooked. But it's coming to the forefront. As it is identified for what it is, as you read, you begin to see, "Oh, that's what that was or is what I experienced." It is like diagnosing a problem and coming to a solution that was always there but was obscured in mimicking something else. Deception and manipulation are present with this spirit. It is one of those things that make you go, "Hmm." So that's what this is as you recognize the way it has presented itself in your life, now as well as in the past.

This is not an exhaustive study concerning this spirit, but it will cause you to seek God even the more to see if this spirit, the Luciferian spirit, has been an operation in your life, is currently operating in your life, and is the root cause of some of the issues that you have had in your life as a Christian and especially as a prophet.

Keep an open mind as you read this book. Seek God for wisdom and revelation as you read. And be willing to admit, profess, and confess if this spirit has been in operation in your life or if you have allowed the spirit to operate in you to cause division with your brothers and sisters in Christ.

As you read, allow the Holy Spirit to minister healing in areas of your life that have been influenced by this and any other spirit not of God.

Prophetess Sabina Cox

TABLE OF CONTENTS

INTRODUCTION..1

CHAPTER 1: Is It True? Is The Luciferian Spirit Among
The Prophets?...3

CHAPTER 2: Prophets Cheated Out Of Their Destiny.................10

CHAPTER 3: Who is this Prophet?..18

CHAPTER 4: Prophet Lot...24

CHAPTER 5: Dark Side of A Prophet..34

CHAPTER 6: The Luciferian Spirit And The Silent Rivalry
Among Prophets...48

CHAPTER 7: The Luciferian spirit, Prophets and Generational
Curses..63

CHAPTER 8: The Luciferian Spirit And Prophetic Breaches........70

CHAPTER 9: The Luciferian Spirit Verses The Dead Wisdom
Of A Prophet..82

CHAPTER 10: The Luciferian Shadow versus The Shadow
Anointing...92

CHAPTER 11: The Prophets Safety Rules For The Luciferian
Spirit..102

CHAPTER 12: The Luciferian Spirit, Still Here To Destroy..........112

ABOUT THE AUTHOR...121

INTRODUCTION

Many spirits seek to operate, manipulate, and dominate the will of God within a prophet's life. Prophet, hear this loud and clear. There is no spirit like the Luciferian Spirit. The Luciferian spirit seeks to destroy Prophets.

Lucifer and Satan are seen as one. The name Luciferian itself denotes 'an enemy.' The term "Satan" itself was a description of the adversary of God. Prophet, the Luciferian spirit is not our friend. This spirit operates on different levels and platforms within the Prophetic Community.

What's funny is that we don't hear much about this spirit compared to the Jezebel Spirit, Jealous spirits, and other demonic entities. This spirit is elite, and make no mistake about it. Deception and behind-the-back covert actions are just some of the special traits of a Luciferian Spirit. The origin of this spirit is derived from satan himself. He is the master of cloche and dagger operations, so keeping his identity silent would be in his favor. The ability to seek and destroy Prophetic operations is priceless to him.

While the Luciferian spirit is a most dangerous spirit for new and emerging prophets especially, this book will also seek to shed light not only on that but also on senior prophets who are falling victim to this heinous entity.

The prophetic demonic assignment of this spirit is devastating to the growth and birth of the Prophet and all Seers. We will explore the origin and introduce some of the dangers of this spirit and what it seeks to destroy within the prophetic realm.

My goal is that God flows through the message of this book. The goal of helping others as we build the kingdom of God is the same as establishing the Prophetic. The purpose of this book is that you become better equipped to deal with this demonic field general on assignment to destroy the prophetic and apostolic by any means necessary.

Let's keep in mind that the Luciferian spirit is at loose, and it seeks to demolish the body of Christ and the prophetic community is the Number one entity on his hit list. Let's now get into the specifics of what I believe is the greatest threat to the Prophetic Spectrum and the Prophetic Community of God's Prophets.

CHAPTER 1

IS IT TRUE? IS THE LUCIFERIAN SPIRIT AMONG THE PROPHETS?

Let's read *Isaiah 14:12-14*. These scriptures read about how thou fall from heaven. The word refers to Lucifer, who is referred to as the son of the morning! The thought of his deception, how he plans to exalt his throne, as he has spoken in thine heart.

Notice he did not speak it out to God but had it in his heart. The book of Isaiah presents us with a vivid biblical narrative. Here, we see the fall of the King of Babylon as it is connected to Satan's rebellion against God. Lucifer was once a beautiful angel of light, but no more.

He now desires to ascend to the highest heaven and exalt himself above God. Lucifer's pride is evident, and that pride and ambition ultimately lead to his downfall. This is what has turned him into the total embodiment of evil.

Lucifer's goal of being in heaven and taking what God had established failed as he was kicked out of heaven. Lucifer wanted to ascend into heaven and be the highest over God. His goal of exalting his throne above the stars of God was futile. Can you imagine this, how messed up and evil the world would be, more than it is now for sure?

I for one, as a student of the prophetic, have dwelled on the fact that he says he sought to be like the highest. Consider that he had no agenda except that what he learned from the highest. He had known absolutely nothing and the fact is that all he learned, he learned from God, and chose to exalt himself above God. Sounds so much like so many of the now-generation prophets.

This is what we see in the prophetic when a prophet comes and knows nothing or very little. The Prophet then learns some concepts and then in a season of time, the Prophet wants to exalt their self above the one who has poured and taught that Prophet. Sit down and talk to prophetic leaders who have labored and listened to the battles they have had with this spirit.

This is the Luciferian spirit; it is the most dangerous spiritual manifestation of the Devil. There is a reality that many Prophetic leaders may not initially discern the Luciferian spirit.

Sometimes, it is not discerned until years of experience and a word of knowledge are deposited within your soul. We may or may not want to admit this fact, but we all surely need to learn of this spirit. It is important to the entire prophetic community to get more of God, as we discern this spirit. To experience this is to remember it.

Within the prophetic realm, this spirit will mainly focus on Sons and daughters of a prophetic heritage to move them and lead them astray. This spirit attacks subordinate leaders and leaders of all levels within the prophetic.

We see the model of the Luciferian spirit in scripture as we look at *Isaiah 14:12-14*. This spirit is modeled here and like Lucifer himself and the King of Babylon, it exhibits a strong and bold spirit that seeks to elevate itself, as it draws comparisons of being equal and above God.

This spirit poisons your mind and makes you think you have done something that you have not. This spirit will elevate you in your mind and set you up for failure and destruction. How many times have you seen this in the prophetic, over and over again?

This is critical that new and emerging prophets especially understand. This spirit will suffocate your growth and fool you into thinking, things about yourself things about other prophets and especially your leaders and it will take you out of the will of God.

Let me explain. Within the prophetic, God has spiritual specialists who he has gifted with special gifts within the prophetic. Many times they may be called to teach, instruct, and activate prophets, while they also maintain standards and feed senior prophets whom God is using in the vineyards. We look at these prophets as establishers, who may become Apostles because of their individual gifts.

God uses them to activate other prophets into the prophetic. Let's Look at the example of a prophetic son or a prophetic daughter who has been raised up and as they are raised up, they are now operating within a level of notoriety they are unaccustomed to. This is not new, but keep reading.

What makes this interesting is that they start to feel themselves as a prophet of great substance, equal to their leadership, who is mentoring them and constantly imparting within them. Right here, go back and look at *Isaiah 14:14* again. They compare and contrast and feel superior to their leadership.

Lucifer said that he would not only exalt his throne above the stars of God, but he had the nerve to say that he was alone. He claims that he will also sit upon the mount of the congregation and be the highest.

Matthew 10:24-26 says that a student is not greater than his teacher. We also see that the servant is not above his master. The student is to share in the teacher's fate. This means that the student should be trained and able to emulate the work of the teacher. We see that Jesus emphasized this point to his disciples and his students.

The servant in this case should have been Lucifer, but we see, that did not work out. The issue here is that Lucifer's plot was revealed, and the issue of his secret plan became public information. We benefit greatly from this disclosure. God already knew what he was going to do and what was going to happen. Prophetic leaders, senior prophets, and Apostles, the closer you walk with God, the more you will appreciate this very fact.

Some critics will tell you that the Luciferian spirit does not exist at all. Does that sound funny and strange to you, Prophet? This is just so tragically strange that it is hard for some prophets to believe that Lucifer works within the system of God wherever he sees an opportunity.

This has to reflect on the teaching they were raised in or the norms within the system they have been raised in. Make no mistake, the Luciferian system has established a belief system that generates the characteristics of Lucifer himself. Do not be fooled, Prophet. I hold, not only to that notion, but many leaders, especially those in the prophetic have been attacked by the spirit. I also say that this spirit is alive and well today.

The very term "Lucifer" is derived from Latin, meaning a light or morning star. The term is associated with the Greek word light bringer. We are talking about the prince of evil spirits, the adversary of God himself. What would make you think that as a spokesperson for God, Lucifer would want to be your friend?

The Luciferian spirit has an assignment to choke and cheat the Prophet out of experiences related to the call upon their life. We will talk about in the next chapter that when this spirit is upon you every-body will be your adversary, especially the leadership who births you.

The Luciferian spirit must exalt itself over everything and every-one. This is the only thing that will give it peace. This is the influence of the Luciferian Spirit among the prophetic. The influence is wicked and deceptive, to say the least.

An illustration and trait of the Luciferian spirit is reflected in *Matthew 13:57*, where Jesus says a prophet is not without honor in his own country. This is the Luciferian spirit in action. It is always unwilling to believe that God has sent you. It is unwilling to recognize you or the authority you walk in. This spirit will not acknowledge you because it will be too familiar with you.

Jesus was not honored as he only laid hands on a few people, who believed and he left. How many prophets have had to deal with this? We all know how we are looked at and reflected upon in our respec-tive areas and circles. Each one of us needs to take a self-test.

I hope by now you can see this spirit in action within the prophetic community. It has been around us for quite some time and has never ceased with its ill will. Look at the self-righteous spirit effect of it. We do see this in the prophetic quite a bit, and it has been a nuisance for quite some time.

In *Numbers 12*, the older sister of Moses and the older brother of Moses are talking about the personal life of Moses as he is doing the work of God. Prophets, beware of those who only focus on your personal life as you do the work of God. Know the Luciferian spirit. The spirit exhibits a self-righteous side that is strong-willed, extremely stern, and very judgmental.

Can you picture being there with Miriam and Aaron and see and listen to them talk about Moses? They are no different than when people who know us talk about us behind our backs. This is especially true when God is using us more than them in their eyes. This very concept demands our attention.

Prophetic leaders, let me say, "Yes this spirit is in your midst and you need to identify it." This is not to say that every time one of your prophets has an opinion or perception different from yours, they are affected by the Luciferian spirit. That is not true.

Prophetic leaders please do not take that approach, but learn who your people are and how to allow them to operate in their gifts as they learn how to respect and honor you for the work that you have been blessed by God to do.

Prophetic leaders, let me say this: you need to be aware of this spirit and not ignore it. You must approach subordinate prophets in a certain way when dealing with this spirit. Philippians 1:9 gives us insight as Apostle Paul says I pray, that your love may grow more in knowledge. He is talking about leaders who know how to love, and it is that love that allows them to discern various spirits.

A study of his work with the Philippians reveals this very fact. Paul taught them how to love and walk in the fruits of righteousness.

Let's be clear, that love, knowledge, and discernment are the friends of the Prophetic leader. This is so especially true for the prophetic leader of today.

CHAPTER 2

PROPHETS CHEATED OUT OF THEIR DESTINY

Let me tell you a story of a prophet who experiences changes in his life. Please understand this can be a male or female prophet. The prophet accepts the leadership of a senior prophet. There is nothing wrong as they will work hard, follow directives, study, sacrifice, and give. The process of development, growth, and maturity has started.

Time passes and the prophet becomes known to be a part of that prophetic group. The identity of this prophet is being birthed. The same prophet over time is given more and more responsibility and even gains some notoriety. There are even times when the prophet is complimented and singled out for outstanding work. This is where we must observe closely.

The same prophet may become more and more familiar with their leadership. This prophet is trusted and feels they know the leadership well. There may be times when they are called upon to be an example to other emerging prophets. Keep looking closely as we start to see a genesis of the spirit form.

The same prophet may be looked upon as a leader and treated as such. As I stated earlier, sometimes it can take prophetic leaders time to see the trend and work of the Luciferian spirit.

How many times have we looked at that prophet and said they were immature? Maybe we spoke about their being unteachable and used similar terms to describe that prophet. Yes, there were scuttle changes started to take place within the prophet's life.

Sometimes they are personal or ministry changes that affect the whole person of the prophet. This can vary from prophet to prophet.

The humility disappears and there is a change from being humble and grateful to being arrogant and prideful, bringing confusion, lies, and chaos that's what this spirit will do. This is not about being fair. It is about the damage that can be done to the emerging or even senior prophet.

While the prophet is still in a learning phase, the anxiousness of that prophet is driven by this spirit to show out and self-elevate them-self. The dangerous work of the Luciferian Spirit is at work. The reality is that this prophet stopped developing and now wants to lead.

The Luciferian spirit will swell and blow your head up. What you need to see here is that the Luciferian Spirit takes control of the next level of the prophet's growth and smothers it.

The same prophet who was up and coming among his peers has been attacked by the Luciferian spirit, and the changes start and mani-fest in a deliberate pattern of disrespect and destruction. Let me be clear. Some leaders will notice this before other leaders.

They will now go behind the prophetic leader's back, like the Absalom spirit, and now explains the faults of the prophetic leader. This prophet, in their newfound wisdom now reinvents the training and methods of his prophetic leadership just like satan did as he attempted to elevate himself and make things better than God did.

This prophet will stumble as they attempt to hide their newfound revelation, as the Prophetic leadership may or may not know something is wrong. This is why communication and education are critical within the spectrum of the prophetic.

Do you remember Gehazi? He was Elisha's trusted servant, and his familiarity with his position caused him to criticize Elisha and eventually betray him. *2 Kings 4:27* is the story of the Shunammite woman and the raising of her son from the dead.

The story of *2 Kings 5* presents us with a classic example. We also see Gehazi go behind Elisha's back when Elisha would not accept an offering from Naaman. This was after Naaman was healed. Also, notice in *2 Kings 4* that Elisha did not initially respond to Gehazi's rant when he could not raise the son up. What is going on with his servant, Gehazi?

Let's start with the fact that Elisha did not accept his offering. The seed was contaminated because Naaman did not believe. Now once he was healed, he was ready to sow into the anointing of Elisha. Elisha makes a point of not accepting the seed because of Naaman's unbelief.

Gehazi does not understand and goes behind his back to accept the seed and curses himself and also his family. This is a betrayal spirit. This is the second time he has gone behind Elisha's back. The Luciferian spirit will always betray its leader.

You will know this spirit as it swears allegiance to a leader and then works in darkness and behind the back of that leader. How many Apostles and Prophets have seen this over and over again?

Gehazi is cursed by Elisha and is now exposed to leprosy and his family descendants are cursed by leprosy also, because of his greed which was fueled by the Luciferian Spirit. Prophets, do not make the mistake of thinking you could not be a victim of the Luciferian Spirit.

Prophetic leaders, while we may attribute it to a bad day or a temporary personal issue, we must be careful and monitor the growth of this behavior. Study Elisha and other senior prophets to see how this spirit is handled. I am a firm believer that there is much that we can learn from each other, especially when it comes to dealing with prophetic personnel issues.

The Luciferian spirit hides so many times as the prophet infected is now choking upon his or her own self-appointed wisdom. Today there seems to be no shortage of that. The Luciferian spirit does not want the prophetic to grow; that is a fact.

The number of prophets, who are painfully like Gehazi in *2 Kings chapters 4 and 5* is astonishing. How do you walk with a leader of that status and still carry a spirit that will betray the prophet? Are you able to see this?

The Luciferin spirit makes prophets unaware of how things are done and most of all, why they may be done that way. Look again. He walked closely with Elisha, so no one is exempt. We must stay in prayer.

I often wonder why Gehazi did not understand the prophetic taxis, which is the mode or way a prophet or a prophetic group operates. Like Gehazi, this type of prophet under this spirit feels they do not need to confer with their prophetic leaders as they may have once did, but not now.

The issue is still the same today as we have become comfortable. Have you ever planted a seed in the ground, but it does not grow comfortably? The seed grows down first and then it grows up and out.

The issue here is that growth is not comfortable, but when we want to be so comfortable that we feel we can do and say anything and it's ok, then we have trouble.

The Luciferian spirit is a spirit that brings trouble to an individual prophet and many times they know not why. Sitting and conferring with the leader seems to be nonexistent. The Luciferian spirit is an enemy of the emerging prophet.

Understand what I have just described is real. Your situation may not be exactly like that but understand how the prophet changes or has changed. The growth of that prophet stops and now an elevated sense of value is upon them. Their head is swollen, in other words.

This is the prophet who was once humble and hungry and is now boastful and full of strife. This prophet now goes against the very leader or leaders who spiritually birthed him.

Notice who this spirit will attack, the emerging prophet mostly, the one who is still developing. The ego and demonstration of pride are now the calling card of that prophet.

You find these prophetic sons and daughters who believe in themselves for elevation rather than the God and His given leadership who has birthed them in the prophetic. In the world, we call this biting the hand that feeds them. The concept is not new, especially in the prophetic ministry circles.

A prophetic son or daughter is precious. *Proverbs 12:15* speaks to us about being teachable and having the ability to take correction. Real sons and daughters in the prophetic are able to demonstrate *Proverbs 12:15* because they honor and respect the position the prophetic affords them through and by God.

The reality is this prophet has choked themself to a prophetic death. They have defiled God's leadership and in their zeal, they have dishonored themselves. In Gehazi's case, they have now corrupted their family lineage. This is the work as they are victims of the Luciferian spirit.

Prophetic leaders, you must identify this type of prophet, within your life. You must understand that this type of prophet will not ever agree with anyone who disagrees with them. This can also happen to leaders.

I have seen some prophetic leaders who become arrogant themselves to deal with, as a replica of the Luciferian spirit. While I feel we all have, notice that this is their way of coping and dealing with this spirit. There are times as a prophetic leader, you must be firm, but at all times, you must be able to work and communicate in love. This will defeat this spirit.

Unless you do the needed work, prophetic leaders, your prophets will never learn how to deal with people and prophetic peers who, come from different cultures, nationalities, countries, and states. This is the shame and they are being cheated out of their destiny.

Can you understand how uncertainty will drive a prophet to become a nomad within their own circles because of their character and demeanor? They are so unstable until you see various changes in their life that have them looking totally different. We see other prophets shy away from them and sometimes even leaders also.

Who is this prophet? You ask? They are arrogant, unstable, and unpredictable. Well who are they, as you may ask again? Let's you and I discuss this more in chapter #3 because it is of critical importance.

Just because a prophet is gifted does not mean that they will accept the responsibilities of the prophetic office. The reality is that a prophet who has their personal life in order is better to work with than a prophet who has a great gift and personal life out of order.

The essence here is that we must use and have love and discernment to deal with this spirit and to continue to grow in the prophetic. My prayer right now is that you have been able to see this spirit as it may exist in your prophetic circles, know how to identify it, and how it is defeated.

On that note, we must talk about the individual prophet and what we can expect from them when this spirit manifests. Scripture has shown us why; now let's see how it affects the individual prophet, seer, or watchman.

There is a reality I feel we must understand and that is this spirit, the Luciferin spirit will choke and cheat a prophet or prophetess out of their destiny. This is why a prophetic leader must also focus on their self-development. It is important to become the best version of ourselves.

CHAPTER 3

WHO IS THIS PROPHET?

1 Thessalonians 5:12-13 says, *"And we beseech you, brethren, to know them which labor. Those who are among you, and those who are your leaders in the Lord. You are to esteem and honor them very highly in love for their work's sake. And be at peace among yourselves."*

The Luciferian spirit goes against this totally in a prophet's life. This prophet has a false sense of security, and maybe the worst thing that happens to prophets is they fail to see their mistakes when operating under the spell of this evil spirit.

Who are they and how do we identify them? Are there any signs you ask? The answer is yes. Let's explore them and understand that our discernment skills will be tested.

Signs of a prophet who has their personal life in order are evident by how they conduct themselves in affairs of personal family responsibility, and how they treat others who may not carry the influence they carry. Prophet, can you clearly answer this question?

Am I talking about you here? Examine yourself, as I could be. Do you just hang to get what you can get and then leave and nothing changes within you?

Prophet, all you do is come to minister and you have no relationship in place or seek to be established prophetically. Your gifts have opened the door, and your arrogance and self-elevation will shut the door.

Prophet, how do you handle your personal financial affairs? Do you sow into the work of God or do you gripe, moan, or complain always when it comes to your giving? All of a sudden you may not believe in giving, so you now gripe echoes of doubt, where there once was faith.

What is funny is that this prophet was once a giver and now things changed as they mumble and grumble about the standard lie about prophets, especially about senior prophets and prophetic leaders. Surely you have heard them talk about how money-hungry they say we are.

While there is much merit to that statement when put into the proper context, this is not the case. This is the Luciferian spirit at work to destroy financial covenants and stability in the Body of Christ and the Prophetic, especially.

The Luciferian spirit is a crafty and intelligent spirit that seeks to understand and destroy the prophetic operation from within. The spirit simply will not speak it out loud, but they will do a Gehazi, and voice to plant doubt and disbelief when financial responsibility is voiced as a concern of leadership. This prophet will see their way to doubt and unbelief to influence the minds of other prophets. Yes, this is real and it has to be stopped.

Think for a moment. Let's review if we know this prophet or not. We will start with financial covenants. The establishment of financial covenants in the prophetic is part of God's plan for funding the kingdom of God. The root of the idea is that certain individuals are designated to be the exponents of financial prosperity.

The Luciferian spirit normally today starts here and shows itself to be quiet and lethal. Let's look at the prophetic ordination process. You do know this prophet. They are ordained on Saturday, and by Tuesday, they need your contact numbers and everyone else, who you know as they now are needed to go and do what you were doing. Oh, how they rant about God calling them to go and, right now!

They who knew nothing are not subject matter experts on what you do wrong as you have now spent many hours teaching them wrongly. This may sound funny, but it is true.

You are training them, but that has officially stopped as they now are ordained by you, prophetic leader. Let you and I remember, "I will exalt my throne" and they do, as it is now suddenly revealed in their actions, and general demeanor.

This goes along with the sudden instant blast of knowledge and wisdom they now have. As you read this, I challenge you to identify that prophet in your life. You better, for your own saneness.

While we discuss that prophet, there is yet another prophet we need to identify as we discuss the Luciferian spirit. You know this prophet also. They float from place to place and complain about why pastors, previous and ex-prophetic leaders, and even Apostles will not allow them to prophesy. They come with excuses and hidden trouble. We will discuss this prophet in another chapter in more detail.

Prophet, I am not suggesting this be true of every prophet that fits this description, but this is the mode that they will operate under until they are exposed. This makes it bad for prophets who have their hearts in the right place before God, and search for a prophetic home.

I find that most prophetic leaders will find ways to excuse themselves from the Luciferian spirit-infected prophet because of the disrespectful nature of that prophet and their desire to protect the other prophets who may be in that prophetic group.

This is why, so often we see it not really taken into consideration that they may not be trained in basic prophetic protocol. This hurts the prophetic and prophets overall when we see this prophet entering a church or assembly where you're not known.

Their untrained conduct seems to always reveal itself. This is why disrespect will bring a prophet the revealing ability to miss out on needed prophetic lessons and training necessary for the function of prophetic taxis or operations. Look at a lot of our peers and you will see the missed lessons by their disrespectful conduct. Consider the work of the Luciferian spirit.

They simply do not know who they are, but the only thing that matters to them is that they are prophets; as they say, God has given them a word. They need to be allowed to operate as they will because of who they proclaim they are.

They fail to realize that the same God who they say has given them this word is a God of order. The Luciferian spirit has robbed them as prophets of character, which is the true identity of a prophet, and when that happens, the maturity of the prophet is nonexistent. Make some mental notes here as you think about this.

So who is this prophet? They are someone who is searching for sure. They are the ones who always boast of what God has told them to do and to be, but they are also the ones who will not submit to anyone, or if they do, it is halfway at best.

Let's be real clear: this is personal as well as demonstrating and being an exponent of the gift. Consider the characteristics of these prophets as we discuss and talk about the Luciferian spirit within the prophetic circles.

Prophets with this spirit will contrast and compare themselves to other leaders as they seek to embarrass and destroy leaders who do not recognize them. Leaders who do not spiritually bow to them are obvious targets.

We can see them as they appear to be angry within themselves. Question: what makes a prophet get ordained, and almost immediately they move forth and try to take over the very ministry they were trained in? Then, when they can't take it over, they are subject matter experts on what is wrong with it.

I have even seen this prophet tell the leaders, who trained them, that they, the leaders need training. This prophet is clearly out of order. We also refer to this prophet as a *Prophet Lot-type prophet*, as I will discuss in chapter 4.

Trust me. This is real and it happens, especially with the prophets, whom one may feel that a Prophetic leader has an easygoing disposition in their mentorship and leadership style. The variance in leadership styles will dictate how vicious the attack of the Luciferian spirit may be through a prophet.

There is no doubt that when the Luciferian spirit attacks a prophet, the prophet will be changed. What is sad is the fact while attacked, they can never be a true prophetic son or daughter, in the sense of real prophetic relations.

This prophet now becomes a victim of the demonic attack and many times, will change the very face of that ministry. The leaders now become extremely agitated with any signs of individuality. While this may vary from leader to leader, it is a result of the fallout of the Luciferian spirit.

Many times, prophetic leaders fail to see prophets or notice the infected Luciferian Prophet until something happens of significant issue. The fact that the infected prophet simply has far too much pride, may not be noticed.

The prophet may, in reality, not want any type of relationship because they will not trust anyone. Let me explain. Let's look now in the public forum to get a hand on how this prophet will act in the private sector.

Please understand how serious this spirit is towards your destruction. Allow me to illustrate this through a prophet you should know well if you have served in the prophetic for any length of specific time.

The name is Prophet Lot, and on the surface, he seems to be ignored by the Luciferian Prophet, but be careful because they are one and the same.

CHAPTER 4

PROPHET LOT

There are many things to learn in the prophetic. One of the absolute most important things is learning God's voice in your process of maturing to be effective.

Understanding Prophet Lot is as priceless as understanding when and when not to speak. This is a known fact. Prophet Lot is a manifestation of the Luciferian spirit. Make no mistake about it. The very name of "Prophet Lot" is a symbolic name of specific actions that will destroy you in the Prophetic. This is the reality of Luciferian empowerment.

Your personal Prophet Lot will demonstrate action that speaks clearly if the prophet is mature or needs to mature. This is why and how the Luciferian attacks emerging prophets, especially.

Prophet, your understanding of Prophet Lot will open or close doors for you. This is an everyday meeting expression of the Luciferian spirit sent to prophetic meetings to destroy the raising up of prophets.

Understanding Prophet Lot is extremely important to your development and Prophet Lot will also figure prominently in your associations and covenant partners. Prophet Lot is not your buddy, friend, or covenant partner.

Genesis 13-19 is the foundation we see in the saga of Lot as the story unfolds. He is the nephew of God's first Prophet, Abraham. We hear so much about his wife, who looked back when God told them not to look back.

On the verge of Sodom's destruction, she looks back and is turned into a pillar of salt. What does all this mean for you as a prophet? Let's discuss that.

The ability of a prophet to grow is directly congruent to their attachment to where that prophet is. In other words, do you know what you gave up? Has your personal Prophet Lot been discarded? The Luciferian wants you to take what you did not work for.

The spirit will use the prophet Lot to accomplish that. The work that is necessary to put a school of the prophets together or a prophetic conference and then there is a prophet there who is out of order, constantly in the bathroom, the parking lot and the restaurant, and even in the meeting, undermining you as they prophesies out of order. The words and information they share are damaging to your cause or meeting.

This prophet easily becomes your biggest critic. This prophet being gifted does not matter, as they are out of order. This prophet wants to exalt their status above where they see yours at. They choose to do it at your expense.

To get personal, prophet, what are you willing to leave behind in your life? What are you willing to let go of totally to move into a life-changing way action for God? Can or are you willing to discipline yourself? And resist this enemy, so he will flee.

God spoke to Abraham and told him to look out as God wanted him to see a vision he could not afford. Abraham had to let go of Lot. God has no respect of person and he wants us to see a vision that we can't afford to miss.

God will not compete with Prophet Lot when he intends to expose his prophet to a global mandate with a global anointing. You must not blow this off. You must understand this.

Those of you reading this and who have been called to the Nations, you must identify the warfare connected to your life and deal with it accordingly.

Many times, we describe Prophet Lot as being so familiar with a prophet until that prophet feels the need to bring Lot into their future. This is a mistake. We can't feel we can pull people where they have no intention of going.

Prophet Lot is destructive, and he is a manifestation of the Luciferian spirit. Notice the submission of a Prophet Lot to the Luciferian spirit as they carry the assignment out to the letter.

Prophet Lot has the ability and gifts of the biblical figure named Lot. What am I telling you? This prophet is selfish and makes sinful decisions without considering the will of God. This prophet is gifted but is world-based and will submit to the will of the world, rather than the will of God.

You must understand that Prophet Lot is gifted and Prophet Lot can manifest into a habit or many times a custom or tradition that we are so familiar with and we feel we have to keep attached to us.

This is the Luciferian spirit as we so often experience within the prophetic so many times. The disobedience of this prophet sometimes will be contagious to this prophet or that prophet.

God may have decided to separate this prophet from our lives and we never realize it. This is why we need to ask ourselves, what's in your life today, right now that will defy God and yet you keep holding on to it? We must eliminate the influence of Prophet Lot. That is not open for debate.

The prophet and the prophetic world, status, and community are different. The life of today's prophet bears witness to that very fact. We are not normal and no matter how hard you may try, we are not called to fit in. We are called to establish the fit for God.

This is why your willingness to let go of Prophet Lot is critical. We may want to feel good about ourselves, but it is more important to deal with our personal Prophet Lot and feel uncomfortable. This I have found is critical to understand.

So what's important in this now day and time we live in? The same important thing then is important now. Godly communication cannot be overstated and so few and far between we see it displayed.

How much do we love Prophet Lot versus our relationship with God? We will never be able to see some things because of our zeal to hold on.

Self-exams start now prophet. Who is your audience Prophet? As we look at Prophet Lot, we should see that the audience will make or break us? Think about this as you reflect on the ways of the Luciferian spirit.

Your audience is the people you talk to and complain to. Your audience is the ones who you confide in. Your audience is the ones who think as you do and ultimately communicate your values. This is a group shot of your Prophet Lot, under the control of the Luciferian spirit who seeks to rise against you.

This is the work of the tag team manifestation of the Luciferian Spirit and Prophet Lot. When you accept their behind-the-back smear campaigns, the griping and moaning, you become just like them.

They are like you. They identify with you. What and who in your audience is in agreement with you and about what? Does it line up with God's order or does it break God's order?

The bottom line is that if you are comfortable and you trust your Prophet Lot, you don't trust God enough to enlarge your ministry and your call into a larger, more diverse spectrum. Who among us is comfortable with your personal Prophet Lot? Are you willing to change?

Change is a hard item to process in the life of a prophet or seer. As we examine Lot, we see he preferred the familiar. While he was taught to trust God, his reasoning was bad for him and his family.

Abraham is his mentor, but like so many of today's prophets who do not want to be mentored, he actually settles for less in his life. Then spends precious time complaining about it to your private audience. Know this: your personal Prophet Lot is a secret agent for the Luciferian spirit.

Lot seems to always have a problem that we see today and that is understanding a life-altering word from God is just that. When God brings a prophet into your life to impart, how many times do you run from the challenge of that prophet?

This is extremely hard for the Luciferian spirit to deal with. Remember, it wants change, but it wants change its way and not the way of God.

Read this Prophet and reflect. Do you pick and choose what you will or will not do? Do you whisper behind your leader's back about the directives?

Do you mumble about what they give you that comes from God? This will be a problem because when God has a desire to move you from your Prophet Lot, you will not move because it is too uncomfortable.

How many of us would rather stay with our Prophet Lot and be comfortable? The issue is that when Lot was removed God spoke to Abraham. Being out of your comfort zone is the greatest thing that can happen to you.

You must leave the clutches of Prophet Lot. That means you're out of the click. You're out of the gossip group on social media, and you are not in the text list or the in-crowd anymore. Yes, they are talking about you. Yes, they are degrading your character, and while it is uncomfortable, this is where God wants you to be.

Are you trusting God or Prophet Lot? Prophet Lot has you in a place of comfort and has surrounded you with other prophets going nowhere and making themselves feel good about each other.

God has you connected, but He is giving you directives through your leadership, which may make you think they are crazy because it involves you being in a position or areas that you are uncomfortable in, and God says, "Trust me. Allow me through your leaders to prepare you for greatness."

Look at the conflict of Lot above his own family; *Genesis 13:6, 7.* Abraham and Lot each had land. The land could not support them while they stayed together, for their possessions were so great.

They both owned large herds and flocks. Quarreling broke out between Abram's herdsmen and the herdsmen of Lot. Abraham said to Lot, "You choose the left or the right and I'll go in the opposite direction." He gave the first preference to Lot.

Lot saw the plain of the Jordan, well-watered like the garden of the Lord. Lot chose the East and lived near the cities of Sodom and Gomorrah.

Genesis 13:13 tells us about the men of Sodom. They were wicked and were sinning greatly against the Lord. Eventually, Lot moved into the city of Sodom with his family, while Abram lived in the hilly area to the west. He becomes invested in the company that he was keeping.

The company that kept him away from God. Are you invested in your Prophet Lot and is the company of Prophet Lot keeping you away from God?

Today, we have so many prophets, who will not leave Prophet Lot because they trust Prophet Lot more than they trust God. Let's look closer into another phase of Prophet Lot. Prophet Lot will always attempt to develop a coup within the ministry. Prophet Lot follows his leader, the Luciferian spirit well. The coup will attempt to raise up its mantle against the leadership mantle.

Prophet Lot always wants a position to influence and direct their agenda outside of the prophetic leadership. Prophet Lot is the gifted Jezebel or Ahab, like the anointed Absalom, who always speaks not to you, but to your people. Prophet Lot, the Luciferian manifestation, is extremely well-versed and a subject matter expert on what leadership is doing wrong.

The Luciferian manifestation of Prophet Lot known as "The Parking Lot Prophet," will always attempt to re-prophesize or belittle the prophetic word or leadership directive from God.

How many times has someone stopped you in the parking lot or spoken to you because God gave them a word and they had to give it to you?

This was because leadership would not let them prophesy. They want to give you what God was really saying because Prophet Lot hears from God. Maybe for you, it was in the bathroom or the hallway and you were approached by Prophet Lot. Trust me it will override or cover what the prophetic word did not do in the meeting.

Another manifestation and cousin of Prophet Lot sometimes will be in the meeting as the Prophet of God is praying and then this special Prophet Lot will start praying with people and laying hands within the crowd of people.

This special Prophet Lot loves to start a prayer line within the meeting to draw attention to themselves. Yes, while the appointed prophet is ministering.

Can you see how this manifestation will scream, holler, and speak what they communicate as what God is saying? All this as they represent the posture of being out of order.

They desire to be a disruptive force in your ministry and your meetings. God is a God of order. *1 Corinthians 14:33* says that our God is not the author of confusion. He is the God of peace, as in all churches of the saints.

What am I saying is that when Prophet Lot is around, God is not there. When Prophet Lot leaves, we can hear from God and experience God. Prophet Lot does not honor protocol. Prophet Lot only honors Prophet Lot.

This is why God does not participate in your life when you are connected to Prophet Lot. This is not about how you shout, speak, or pray. This is about who has the honor in your life. Who you listen to controls your ear and controls your destiny.

The process of allowing God to control your destiny is a soul function that has to be practiced and learned and then practiced again for the unseen, the unknown. You can't afford to allow Prophet Lot to officiate in your life.

Prophet Lot is your gossip partner. They are always looking to control everything including you, the leader. Prophet Lot wants to make you spend more time dealing with their nonsense than becoming the Prophet and leader that God has called you to be. Prophet Lot is gifted but not gifted to be your friend.

The problem with Prophet Lot is that they could be family. They could be your biggest supporter until they believe they have a better way.

Prophet Lot may have started with you, but along the way, Prophet Lot assumed your position because of a lack of understanding relationships. Prophet Lot has become your biggest obstacle and many times you may not know it. Do you understand that Prophet Lot is your one-way ticket to being in covenant with the Luciferian spirit?

This is why relationships among prophets should not be abused or taken for granted. Prophetic relationships are earned. They are not handed out.

Prophet Lot does not understand that prophetic relationships are built on honor and respect. When Prophet Lot leaves your life, God will speak.

Abraham learned that his biggest obstacle was Lot, his nephew, who would not listen. His nephew had a better way than God. The people around you as a prophet will determine who you are. They will determine how high you will go in God.

Are you willing to leave your life in the hands of your Prophet Lot? God tells Abraham to look out from where you are. Are you willing to look globally? Prophet Lot will blind you to a global vision. The only thing that will be revealed is your dark side, prophet.

This manifestation of the Luciferian spirit is alive and well. Let me now discuss the Dark side of a prophet and see the marriage it represents with the Luciferian spirit. Just like Prophet Lot, God wanted Abraham to look at a vision he could not afford to miss. Look to a vision that only God can allow you to experience. Drop Prophet Lot and you will see God in a whole new way.

CHAPTER 5

DARK SIDE OF A PROPHET

The culture of our generation, the society, the norms, and the acceptance are not a spontaneous trend that sprung out of nowhere. Cultural trends are the result of years of various types of influence on the masses of people.

The influence of symbols and messages is clearly evident in any given culture. The Luciferian spirit is a spirit that masters camouflage for the culture and current times.

The Prophet Balaam was a descendant of Shem. Those who knew the Prophet Balaam would see him today in our society as highly anointed and gifted. He is a figure of strength and power; he is symbolic of God's position with Israel and yet today, we see a Balaam who is all that, and they are controversial and shows us the dark side of a prophet inspired by the Luciferian spirit.

The Prophet Balaam was hired to curse Israel, and God turned the curse into a blessing, in light of Balaam wanting to curse Israel, but failing.

In *Numbers 31*, the Israelites killed Balaam when they conquered Midian because the Prophet Balaam incited them to worship foreign gods. What a contrast.

Let's look at the Prophet Balaam. He is a mixture of positive and negative press that is mirrored in the prophetic mantle. He is condemned as evil in *Numbers 22:18* and yet he seems to have been a gifted prophet who is looked upon as a false prophet.

Today, many of you may reach this point and shudder in your growth. Welcome to the *Dark side of a Prophet*. There is an important point for all of us to see here.

Balaam has reached a level of maturity in his ministry and in his life that affords him a level of notoriety because of his prophetic gift. We have to see here, that he has a level of relevance in the prophetic. How do you handle yourself when your gift has positioned you in a place you have never been?

There, however, is more to discuss here. Balaam represents the idea that the motivations and actions of a prophet can align with Lucifer; thus, here is the connection to the Luciferian spirit. This is clear, simple, and yet complicated all at the same time.

The beautiful thing is that God will forever put us in a position where we can grow and learn from. Let's see what happens Prophet when the cheers of man become louder than the voice of God in your life.

This is where Balaam is at, and prophets it is important to take the time and learn why a prophet so gifted is in a situation so unsettling. Prophet, this is where your life will become exposed. This is your dark side and the Luciferian spirit door into your life.

The dark side of Balaam is now on display, and a humbling by God will expose his and our secret issues of personal development that have never developed.

You may be able to hide them and yet now they are exposed before God and Man. This is a wake-up call for mature prophets. What am I saying? I'm saying that the dark side of Balaam and your dark side will be exposed and exposure presents an invaluable life lesson for a prophet.

Balaam is a prophet who has abused his gifts and relationship with God. This is about his personal gain to him. Hopefully, every prophet of God can learn the invaluable lesson that Balaam learned the hard way. The pursuit of personal gain will always be in a battle for obedience to God in a prophet's life.

Consider the following and let's look at this closely. The children of Israel are wandering through the desert, and have just beaten up, killed, and plundered the Amorites.

Balak, the king of Moab, has just seen all of this, and he begins considering what might happen to them! Worried that his people might be next in line for defeat, Balak tries to get some "insurance" by getting God's Prophet, Balaam, on their side.

"So he sends messengers to Balaam saying, 'Behold a people came out of Egypt, and they are living to oppose me. Please come and curse these people for me; perhaps I may be able to defeat them and drive them out of the land. For I know that he whom you bless is going to be blessed and whom you curse is cursed.'" The message of the king of Moab is the very tool God uses to expose the dark side of

his Prophet. This also leads us to understand the application of the Luciferian spirit.

Let's explore 3 things you, as a prophet, must learn to deal with:

1. The reputation of a prophet is...the perception of the Prophet:

Balaam had established a great reputation! Prophets whom God uses will have reputations. This is a fact as people analyze your human traits while they try to see God in and upon you. Learn this. It will help you in your focus.

Balaam was the type of Prophet that if he said a person was blessed, they were really blessed and if he said they were cursed, it was all over for them! After all, who would hire a guy to come and curse their enemies if they didn't think it was going to work?

Understand it would not hurt to read this again as you understand who Balaam was and how he walked as a prophet. There is not an awful lot known about the history of Balaam, but we do know that God speaks to him in this story, and His reputation is known far and wide as a prophet of God. In today's terms, he is established in his mantle.

Balaam is not a novice. Notice here that he is well established, and yet the overtone of the Luciferian spirit is ever present. This is the fight many of today's prophets have but doesn't realize it.

Balaam knows the voice of God and everybody knows that Balaam's gift was accurate and sure. The danger for Balaam was in how he was received because of his gift. He is approached by a man. Who is he really listening to?

Prophets understand that people will want to use your gift for their selfish reasons. Here we see the Luciferian influence. You will be tested in your ability to express and communicate the value of your anointing. This is illustrated in the second point here.

Some of you are wondering why God is allowing you to go through so much because you have been given much, and much will be expected of you!

2. Understanding the Attraction of Earthly Riches

So Balak sent some of his leaders to go see Balaam, and to bring him "fees of divination." Can you imagine how they now came to Balaam? The words of Balak are repeated to him again. He tells them, "Please spend the night here." He says, "I will bring the word back to you as the Lord may speak to me." Notice that he is going to God again after God said no.

God spoke to Balaam and said, "Who are these men with you?" Notice that God asked him, who are these two men? Do you recognize this spirit when you see it? Prophet, do you recognize who and what they should have represented to the Prophet?

Balaam said, "Balak the king of Moab, has sent a message to me again." He now describes the situation. Is it that obvious that he thinks God does not know? He says "Behold, there is a people who came out of Egypt. The king wants him to come and curse them. I may be able to fight against them and drive them out."

Why would God ask his Prophet who are these people? Look closely, prophets. Has God ever asked you a question because He wanted you to see something that you had not? This is so key here!

Balaam has been given an opportunity to identify a concealed presence. This is no different than what we deal with daily and over time and as stated, we may want it, but what if we can't relate to it? Balaam simply can't relate to the issues at work here.

Look at the fact that Balaam was turned away from God by what was put down before him. Also, Balaam had an opportunity to win souls, but he did not.

While we know the Prophet is worthy of his hire, we also can see that Balaam is enticed by the opportunity of earthly riches. There is a responsibility for us to know when God is sending us and when He is not.

Stop and think. Balaam, yourself and I just can't be the only ones who see this and missed it. We have missed the Luciferian overtone for oh so long. It happened then and still happens now today.

Look closer at the enticement of earthly riches. Somehow, we seem to always forget that *Matthew 6:33*, says seek ye first and the needed things of life will be added. This is why we have to be equipped. The kingdom of God is the key to what we need now and will need.

3.   Second Guessing God........No Conviction In your heart

God said to Balaam, "Do not go with them; you shall not curse the people; for they are blessed.'" That's it. Do not go with them. You can't get any clearer than that!

Now, God doesn't always tell you why. Balaam had a good relationship with God, that God told him why he wasn't supposed to go. "You shall not curse the people; for they are blessed." That should have been the end of it for Balaam, but it was not.

We see the following happened. Balaam tells Balak's leaders, to simply, "Go back to your land, for the Lord has refused to let me go with you.' And they went to Balak, and said, `Balaam refused to come with us.'"

The saga continues as I need you to realize that Balaam is a senior prophet, anointed and known for his kingdom work. Yet the Luciferian spirit has approached him for what he has gained in his life work and it simply wants to destroy him. Look at this and see the perspective from all angles.

Balak once again sent leaders. He was determined. These leaders are much more numerous and distinguished than the first group. And they came to Balaam and said to him, "Thus says Balak." The words of Balak are stern as he tells the prophet through his leaders to let nothing hinder him. I beg you, hinder you. He is drawing a line for Balaam to choose from. Will it be him or will it be God? He claims to indeed honor the prophet.

The message is for Balaam: please come and curse these people for me. I really need you Balaam. I have work for you to do. We need you to come and curse these people.

But when Balaam asked God, He said, "No. These people are blessed, and I don't want you to hurt them." The obvious thing for Balaam to have told the messengers would have been, "I can't curse these people because God said they are blessed." The cunning nature of the Luciferian spirit penetrates the very soul of God's anointed prophet.

But what did Balaam say to the messengers? "Go back to your land, for the Lord has refused to let me go with you." What does that mean? He wishes he could go, but "God won't let him."

Remember those "fees of divination?" Balaam got paid for his work. There wasn't anything strange about that in those days. It was customary, as it still is today, to bring a gift when you sought the word of God from a prophet.

Balaam knew there was some big money to be made, and what he was really saying was, "I'd like to go, but I can't." If someone knows that you really want to do something, even if you shouldn't, it will inspire them to keep trying to get you to change your mind.

The Luciferian spirit is cunning and smart. This spirit has mastered the study of man and is skilled at picking out the weaknesses of especially prophets. This spirit will give up if it knows that you are convinced because of strong convictions in your own heart. This is a soul issue that we as Prophet must solve. The issue is cut and dry. We are dealing with a soul issue.

Here is where you should see the Luciferian spirit at work. Prophet if you can't obey with joy in your heart, then you're asking for trouble. If your response is, "Gee, I'd really like to go, but the Lord won't let me," you need to see how wicked that is and realize that you're opening yourself up for all sorts of attacks.

If the devil knows you're convinced that God is the wisest and that you know it's best to follow God's counsel, then he doesn't have a point of attack. I say again the Luciferian spirit is connected to Balaam and our dark sides because he exploits our lack of conviction.

This spirit now has an easy job. All he's got to do is get you to believe that your opinions are better, smarter, or more pleasing than God's principles. There's a big difference between just obeying God on the outside, and obeying with a thankful, joyful, and agreeable heart.

You want to do it your way. Notice that God came to Balaam at night and said to him, "If the men have come to call you, rise up and go with them; but only the word which I speak to you shall you do.'" Now, on the surface, it doesn't seem like there's anything harmful or angry in God's answer to Balaam.

Balaam had asked God once, was told "No," and then asked a second time. Don't ever ask God again once He gives you the final word on something.

He gave Balaam a definite word of no! And He told him why. But Balaam said, "I want to go find out what else." When Balaam came back a second time, God told him what he wanted to hear. "Sure, go ahead." Why? You'll see.

It is morning time now, and now the prophet has saddled his donkey. He now travels, with the leaders of Moab. But God was angry because he was going. Now, why would God tell Balaam to do something, and then be angry when he did it?

Let this be a warning. Unless you understand what Balaam represented to God, it may be hard to see why God was angry. This is how God esteems his prophets. They mean that much to God. The expectations upon our lives are numerous, high, and extremely important.

Prophet, please make sure you remember this. The truth is that God will never tell you to do something He once told you not to do unless He explains why He's changing His path.

Remember this. God told Abraham, "Go offer your son as a burnt offering," but later said, "Do not harm the boy." God said to Abraham, "Now I know you fear Me. You have proved yourself. Abraham, I know you love Me more than anything else *(Gen. 22:2-12)."* God said, "Son, I'm changing My direction, and this is why." You can expect that when you are in a relationship with God.

Let's explore this situation with Balaam even more. Now watch as God says "No" to Balaam one time, and the next time He just tells him, "All right, go," without giving any reason. We all should look at this and beware. The implication is here that something is unspoken as we observe and see God deal with His Prophet.

Prophet God says "No," but you keep asking, so God says, "All right, if you're not going to be obedient, go ahead. Do what you want."

Watch out. There is a separation here. This is what happens with the Luciferian spirit. It positions itself for separation from God. This has happened in the Garden of Eden and every time there is a whining and whimpering to God about something after He's already given you "no" for an answer.

The prophet has to be very careful. God is all-knowing and to think that we have slipped something by God is a joke. You may get what you want, but the results and process may yield some disastrous results like Balaam got. There should be no doubt after reading the previous chapters that God knows who was pushing Balaam.

He is riding on his donkey with the leaders of Moab. There now appears an angel of God as an adversary to Balaam. What's amazing is that the angel is seen by the donkey, but not by Balaam. The donkey turns and goes off into the field, but Balaam struck the donkey to turn her back. Three times this happened. The reality is the donkey saw the angel and got out of the way very fast!

Have you ever wondered why Balaam did not see the donkey? Think about this and understand the scene. Three times he struck his donkey and finally, it just laid down right in the middle of the road. Balaam was angry and now the donkey speaks to him.

The donkey wants to know what is wrong with Balaam because it is only trying to protect Balaam. The animal speaks to him. "What have I done to you, that you have struck me these three times?'" And Balaam is so shocked that he answers it! "Because you have made a mockery of me!'"

He's never been so embarrassed in all his life! The Luciferian spirit will embarrass and humiliate you. "And the donkey said, `Am I not your donkey on which you have ridden all your life? Have I ever been accustomed to do so to you?'"

Now finally, Balaam's eyes are open. You have to wonder how he feels when he sees the angel of God with his sword drawn. The sight had to be simply overwhelming!

Understand that the great Balaam was blind and now he can see. What is important is that the angel said to him, "Why have you struck your donkey?" The angel now explains the situation to Balaam.

Balaam here is experiencing prophetic block, plain and simple. He could have been killed and did not realize it. Prophets, there is a lesson here we all need to learn.

Do you see what God did, so quick and fast to Balaam? His donkey saw the angel and turned aside. If it had not, Balaam may very well have been dead.

God's message to him was, "Your donkey just saved your life. It was trying to keep you out of trouble." Can you think of the things in your life that may have been out of order and because you were determined to go forth, God protected you as He did with Balaam?

A clearly confused Balaam said to the angel, "I sinned." He now says that he did not know about the angel. He even says he is willing to turn back.

Have you ever seen a prophet disciplined within a prophetic group? This is Balaam in this situation being reminded of who he works for. Even while this seems to be apparent, all is still not absolute with Balaam. I wonder why, do you?

The point of this is to see the cunningness of the Luciferian spirit at work. This spirit is deeply deposited within Balaam and upon prophets today.

We look at Balaam. He wants to debate and plead with God's decision, yet once again. Does he not realize that he could have been killed for his disobedience? The significance of the fact is lost to him.

Look at the facts. Your donkey is talking to you, and you've got the angel of the Lord Himself standing before you with a drawn sword telling you that your way is contrary, and you're saying, "If it is displeasing, I will turn back"! Are you kidding? God wrote Balaam off right there.

Do you see his tone and manner are defiant? Remember we have discussed that this spirit is cunning, sneaky, conniving, and deep-rooted. Darkness is its workplace.

Never once did he say, "God, I've sinned." He did not say God allow me to repent. God, you told me not to go, and I'm turning back right now." But he doesn't repent. Spend some time to look at this closely and understand it.

This is how Balaam is acting under the various shades of his dark side. The Luciferian spirit has completely captivated his emotions and we see how he processes the favor of God when he is exposed to it. The reality is there are some prophets you and I know who are just like this. Who am I talking about? Clearly not you, right?

This type of prophetic influence is not new, but it was prevalent then and now in our everyday modern society. Prophets, do you see us? Again, we want to do what we want to do despite what God says.

History has steered us to be shy when dealing with what's been banned in our lives, like the dark realm or demonic spirits. We, the prophets, seem to be very limited in dealing openly and honestly with the dark spirit realm. This is what the Luciferian spirit thrives on.

Satanism is rampant in movies and the influence of the Luciferian spirit is very open in prophetic circles. In *2 Corinthians 2:11,* Paul taught that we should be aware and wary of such dark practices, "lest Satan should take advantage of us, for we can't "stay ignorant of his devices."

The Dark side is the dwelling spot of the Luciferian spirit. Make no mistake about this cloak-and-dagger spirit. Just know it has many vices it will use to destroy you if you're not focused or ready.

Leviticus 19:31 reminds prophets to not give any regard to mediums and familiar spirits. Prophet do not seek after them, and we are not to be defiled by them. This includes the Luciferian spirit especially. We have to know what is God and what is not.

This is so important because some want to separate Lucifer and Satan as being two separate entities. How you view this depends upon your spiritual roots and understanding. Satan is seen as rebellious and confrontational, just as the Luciferian spirit is the unseen manifestation of the satanic mentality.

The characteristics of this spirit, who deals in darkness, trickery, temptation, and destruction, only elevates the ideas and imagery that have risen from his role as satan himself. Balaam walks a fine line in this equation and God demonstrates to him that he is not as smart as he thinks he is. Prophets can you see yourself here? We all need to look for ourselves.

The Luciferian spirit, being an extension of satan himself, presents us with another dilemma. This is one we can't ignore. There is no secret that we all are involved in a silent war. Welcome to the prophetic, as we consider the silent rivalry and war among the prophets, fueled by the Luciferian spirit. This must be discussed.

CHAPTER 6

THE LUCIFERIAN SPIRIT AND THE SILENT RIVALRY AMONG PROPHETS

Philippians 2:2-3 says, *"Complete my joy by being of the same mind, having the same love, being in full accord and of one mind. We are to do nothing to feed a rivalry within the kingdom of God."*

We are to move in humility and honor others. We must stay humble. This is hard to do among prophets, especially when they are gifted and start to feel themselves as important and relevant.

Successful prophets learn how to master this in the art of living. They demonstrate leadership in the way they live and communicate. Leaders pay close attention here. The successful prophets will constantly remind themselves that the beauty of life in Christ is what illuminates the struggle that exists within all of us, the struggle between reason and passion. This is where the Luciferian spirit invades our lives.

This is the place where our soul is open to good versus evil. We are talking about the place where the Luciferian spirit invades us. Our person is changed and our mind is clouded. We now turn ourselves into a puppet with our prophetic gift. This is why our soul does not prosper because it is the place where the Luciferian spirit thrives in our life.

As a prophet, our soul is very often the greatest and most active battlefield, upon which our reason and our judgment wage war in our minds against our passion and our appetite. Think about this: what is your passion for greatness in God, but you're not sure if you have the appetite for that level of success you seek? The issue is not new, not at all.

Can we really turn discord and rivalry into oneness and melody? Blessed are you as the prophet. The prophet that walks not in the counsel of the ungodly.

Prophet you dare not stand with and in the ways of sinners. You constantly delight in the ways, laws, and word of God *(Psalm 1:1-3)*. Prophet, if you're going to be effective, you must have the mentality and be like a tree that will not be moved. This is the war within we have to fight and deal with as we deal with our peers and ourselves.

Prophet, ask yourself, what drives you? Does your passion drive you? What are your reasons? What will move your seafaring soul? Is your soul in need of repair? We can always toss and drift instead of being able to stand still in mid-seas crisis. We must fulfill our life assignment, and many times, it will be dealing with the crisis of life itself. This is a fact.

This also leads us to discover what we refer to as silent rivalry. This is within ourselves and within our ranks. The emergence of the Luciferian spirit is busy at work among our souls and our ranks. Look at the fact that each of us feeds a silent rivalry among our prophetic ranks.

Silent rivalry feeds a multitude of issues in our ministries like jealousy, unhealthy relationships, gossip, racism, and sexism, just to name some of the issues. The reality is that the silent rivalry is so deeply ingrained in our society today that most of us will fail even to recognize it. We seem to think it is the accepted norm. Welcome to the struggle between reason and passion.

Let us recap the Luciferian spirit again. The human imagination is the battle ground within the prophet. This is the meeting place where the clash between good and evil is waged. I have pointed out that the Luciferian spirit embodies rebellion, pride, and the pursuit of personal power. Now, picture this in your mind. The mind is a vital part of the soul.

This now has positioned us as prophets to engage in a silent war among prophets. This is us against us. This is the Luciferian spirit at work. This was true of the biblical days and the now-day contemporary generation.

Prophets, we must come to an understanding of the silent war among prophets as we examine the characteristics of this spirit and its impact on prophetic leaders and prophets.

The Bible also presents instances of a silent war among prophets, wherein true messengers of God encounter opposition from those who have succumbed to the Luciferian spirit. Clearly, we have opposition like that today.

For example, in the Old Testament, the prophet Elijah confronted the prophets of Baal, who worshiped false gods. This clash symbolizes the battle between divine truth and deception, righteousness and corruption. Similarly, in the New Testament, Jesus warned his followers about false prophets who would arise, misleading people and distorting the essence of his teachings. How do we look at this today? Thanks for asking.

The Luciferian Spirit of today feeds the silent war among prophets in our new generation. Prophets and religious leaders grapple with the allure of power, fame, and material wealth. We do ignite rivalries among our ranks. This is not to say that prophets do not serve in their communities because they do. The reality of a lack of honor is real, not imagined.

The reality is that we do have a group of now-generation prophets who will succumb to the Luciferian spirit. We see them using their positions for personal gain or to manipulate others. We call it so many names, but it's the influence of the Luciferian spirit that such individuals may distort religious teachings, promoting division, intolerance, and greed.

We use things like social media to take shots at each other. We have almost lost the ability to empower. The sad part is when we do, it has to be so guarded, or you may risk getting hurt by the Luciferian spirit or one of its imps. This is why our prophetic relationships can be so unstable.

I am totally convinced that the Luciferian spirit is the greatest enemy to the prophetic development of a prophet. The spirit works so undercover and is so diverse and crafty; it is a controller and a shadowing commander of other spirits. The Luciferian spirit is a master demonic craftsman; it pushes many buttons to keep division within the prophetic community.

Today, we see the impact on our society. The consequences are far-reaching. Let's look at the prophets of today and think about how our actions sow seeds of doubt and total confusion. The infected Luciferian prophet has eroded the trust of a fair number of religious institutions and their leaders.

The actions of these untrained and infected prophets have cost the Body of Christ so much. Look at us; we have totally exploited others' vulnerability. We have lacked in our ability to empower. Do you see how our methods of undisciplined leadership have hindered the spiritual growth of so many prophets? We even have people running from the prophetic because of the silent war they want no part of.

Within our ranks, we have division and hostility with churches, ministries, and various religious groups. We need conflict to exist. The ideologies that clash and cause rifts constantly foster a sense of spiritual disarray. I say again, this is the norm. Have you considered that we have no unified training with the prophetic spectrum? We have senior prophets creating manuals from years of hurt, disappointment, frustration, and pain in order to empower emerging prophets.

The struggle is real. You are the mouth piece of God and you must be aware of it. Learn and realize that learning never stops. You, as a prophet, are obligated to keep learning.

Fighting the Luciferian spirit as it feeds the silent rivalry is the perceived, real, or imagined competition for the same objective or for superiority in the same field. The field is the prophetic. The zeal to be effective, known and admired and make plenty of money.

This issue will always exist in some form or fashion until you, your circle of prophets, or your covenant prophetic partners reach a level of maturity that will allow you to experience God in the fullness.

Among our peers and, in our case, prophets, competitive feelings can spark intense rounds of self-reflection. We see someone whose ministry is taking off and then ask ourselves what fatal flaw prevents us from generating the dazzling output they do. Either we think that we're not talented or gifted enough, or, worse, maybe we are too lazy or shy to capitalize on it. Maybe, just maybe God has something else for you to do in a different season just as awesome.

The shame of the matter is that the silent rivalry puts us in a place where petty jealousy thrives and throws our priorities out of order. The Luciferian spirit has separated and destroyed unity as it lurks in the dark background. Look at the Prophetic Community around you, and you know if you need to make some changes. I ask you to be honest with yourself.

Right now, prophet, if you need to, change your perspective and stop telling yourself useful lies to cover up your shortcomings. Many times, as prophets, we seek silence in depression, mood swings, and self-pity as the negative output of waging a silent rivalry thrives. This can be with a peer or peers who we may or may not be in relationship with.

Living out our visions is a tremendous challenge because they represent communications from God and are important to the prophet or seer. Only through and by a relationship with God can we be successful.

One of the darkest sides of a silent rivalry is represented in the person of the prophet Balaam. My prayer is that you saw that in the previous chapter. He clearly has a dark side that wars with his Godly character in what he knows is God and what is not. This is the prophet's inner man at war.

Today, we see this as the supposed prophetic son or daughter speaks to their leaders or how they talk about their leaders. Do they do it with respect and leave no doubt about who they are, or do they speak with the temptation of looking for greener pastures or my leaders are not adequate? I see this over and over at prophetic meetings. Many of us see this over and over again.

There is sadness, shame, and disgust when we see a prophet who is gifted and wages a war within themselves. The prophet is wanting to obey God but wanting to obey God with all the perks and accolades of today's now generation. Like Balaam, so many times we are asked to curse what God had blessed.

Our reward is another booking and the truth be told, it is not worth it. Sometimes, you need to know when to say no. Had Balaam been living today, maybe the process of mindfulness would have been most beneficial to him.

My hope is that he would have had some prophets of his stature that he would have listened to and knew that God had his best interest at heart. This is a serious issue and as leaders, we need to solve it.

Could mindfulness have helped Balaam? I feel it would have. That's only my feeling. It may not be yours. Mindfulness is a social practice of emptying your mind of fears, hates, insecurities, regrets, and guilt.

The generation of Balaam and our now generation may not be synched together, but the issue is interesting to consider. Let's be real, as we look at the relationships with God then and now today. We are still learning, so stay hungry and humble prophets.

Making the effort to empty your mind tends to give relief on troublesome issues of a prophet's everyday life. Balaam would have benefitted from this as many prophets today. The reality of the Luciferian spirit wanting to dominate would be rescinded if we empty our minds and refill our thoughts with the thoughts of God. This is the key that we just don't seem to want to use. This is how we defeat this ministry of torment.

As prophets, we need to be empty in the presence of God and casting our cares upon Him, and allowing Him to fill us up. This, in turn, leads us to develop our gifts in our daily practice. What would it mean to you to be called upon to pray for others, repeatedly and indiscriminately?

Consider what you have read so far on the Luciferian spirit and prophets and think about how you can pray for a stranger you passed on the street, or a person whom you glimpsed briefly out the window of your car.

The thoughts of your mind are critical. The silence we deal with sometimes will have us listening to negative thoughts. This is the work of the Luciferian spirit; it always brings negative energy. Remember the cunning nature of this spirit. Now keep your mind active as you pray for others' good health, prosperity, and a better tomorrow.

Prophet, free yourself of negative energy so you can get some actual work done, at which point you probably won't care so much about what other people are doing. You'll be in the zone. This is how you will learn how to deal with the silent rivalry issues of the influence of the Luciferian spirit. Many prophets, even as you read this are dealing with silent rivalries with yourself or someone - especially a prophet.

Two biblical prophets who really seemed to have had a silent rivalry between them were Ezekiel and Jeremiah. What and why? The uncommon silence? I now open a long-standing question in the study of Ezekiel and his relationship to Jeremiah. Oh my God, how it reminds me of today; let me say amen here.

The silence between the prophets is like a hidden key that needs to be found. The key would open the door to an issue long overdue in the body of Christ: the issue of prophetic relations. Prophetic relations are a real issue that is unstable at best in our generation.

Sure there are remnants, but I ask you to get my book on this issue. The book is called *"Prophet Called to a Cross-Culture."* This topic has to be discussed openly. The issue has been ignored long enough.

The issue so often is why do gifted prophets war silently within their ranks, circles, churches, fellowships, and with each other. The human nature that we blame is the very same human nature we can control if we put the effort in. We must understand who our enemy really is.

We do not understand how to celebrate each other. Our time is spent more in toleration and covering up our inadequacies. When we don't understand that the love we say we have is an action word. Can you see how the Luciferian spirit fits in here?

Looking at Ezekiel and Jeremiah, this is not a secret. Both had a relationship with God, but like today, many prophets will have relationships with God and not each other. Let's wonder about that. How does God feel when He has placed them to work together and empower each other? It's funny sometimes how their spirits will be closed to each other, but open to God. Have you ever wondered about that?

How is it that our working and prophetic relationship building is so difficult, especially when our challenge is to work with someone different and be blessed through and by God? Clearly there is a level of maturing needed across the broad within the prophetic realm of God's prophetically gifted. We all need to do a better job in this arena.

Within our prophetic lineages, many times, we see differences on issues of procedure, issues on protocol, issues of culture, custom and the different layers of society. The silence between Ezekiel and Jeremiah may have covered a great ideological disagreement between the two great contemporary prophets of God.

Hence, the silence between them is an eloquent silence as many of us experience today. How many prophets and people are you silent to on social media, but yet you claim them as a friend? Don't think for one minute the Luciferian spirit wants us to be friends and have real covenant relationships. Let's be real here.

Notice that Ezekiel and Jeremiah are both well know prophets. The time is before and after Judah's destruction. This is also at the beginning of the Babylonian exile. Clearly, we read of these two prophets that they neither spoke of each other by name.

At face value, there would seem to be no problem with the silence maintained between the two prophets. Throughout the prophetic literature, the extremely individualistic nature of the prophetic role seems to work against explicit communication between prophets. Sounds so much like today. What's happening in your prophetic community?

We can look at *Ezra 5:1; 6:14* and see that both Haggai and Zechariah participated in the reconstruction of the Second Temple. Then we look at the School of the Prophet and earlier, the companies of the Prophets; this seems to not fall in line with this way of thinking.

The expectation that some kind of contact existed between Ezekiel and Jeremiah is based on the fact that each of them recognizes their time as a period of intensive prophetic activity, marked by fierce issues over both status and message *(Jeremiah 14:13–16; 23:9–40; 27–29; Ezekiel 13)*. Jeremiah mentions by name some prophets who were active in Babylon *(Jeremiah 29:21, 24)* yet says nothing about that one prophet, Ezekiel.

Jeremiah says, *"The LORD has raised up prophets for us in Babylon" (Jeremiah 29:15)*. The question you want to ask is, is Jeremiah referring obliquely to or putting down Ezekiel? Ezekiel's narrative *(Ezekiel 1:1)* says he was called to his prophetic mission on the Kebar River in Babylon.

Both Jeremiah and Ezekiel have quite similar personal backgrounds, as members of priestly families commissioned to prophesy *(Ezekiel 1:3; Jeremiah 1:1)*. Was there a rivalry between their priestly families since Ezekiel was of Jerusalemite? The issue of a personal issue here is real, while not blatantly expressed.

Clearly that Jeremiah and Ezekiel would not only have known of each other by name, but also would have been aware of each other's prophetic activity. So why is there no praying together, fellowship, or seeking God together? That is a good question. Maybe we should ask ourselves the same question.

Now think about it, and you will know that not much has changed today. Let me ask the question again. Do you feel the Luciferian spirit is within the prophetic community as a whole? Let's ask that same question about what is going on today in ministries. Let me add, let's be real.

Just like Jeremiah and Ezekiel, we see they were not in each other's circles. There is a silent rivalry with in our prophetic ranks today and we know it, but most of us do not know why. So often our silence is a sign of the difference between prophets.

I point this out as an outreach of the Luciferian spirit. This is a specific blanket of influence within the prophetic. We are prophets with specific ministries to specific groups of people. It is strange how we seem to never have any fellowship with some of our peers. Yes, there are reasons and then there are our personal issues.

The Book of Daniel tells us that Daniel was quite aware of Jeremiah's prophecies. While we look at the fact that there is no indication Ezekiel was ever acquainted with Daniel. Ezekiel focuses a good deal of his ministry on God as a Person.

People have called Ezekiel the prophet of the Spirit. People have called Isaiah the prophet of the Son. We also see Jeremiah referred to as the prophet of the Father. These are absolutely relative prophets and would be today also.

Despite what seemed like no contact between the two prophets, Ezekiel confirmed Jeremiah's message. The message was that Jerusalem would be totally destroyed.

They were told to return to God. There would be only a small remand that would return to Jerusalem. A young Ezekiel, during the darkest days of the Jerusalem is focused, but we wonder why the silence?

Ezekiel comes from a pit of slavery to a foreign land to fight against the false hope spewed by what we call false or fake prophets today. He fights against depression and desperation that hurt the hearts of literally all of the people. People who are and were in a total reluctance to accept their own responsibility for their current condition. Clearly this sounds like today in our generation.

Ezekiel 24:24 says, "Ezekiel say to the people, let this be to you a sign. When this comes, then you will know that I am the Lord GOD." Jeremiah says that because of the ways that they ignore justice and the vulnerable, God judged their sinful nation. Jeremiah's message spoke to the contrary, about being led out from Judah as well, into exile and away from all that he knew and loved.

Jeremiah and Ezekiel represent two prophets who fit together because they were both doing God's work simultaneously. Both prophesied around when Babylon was growing in strength as an empire.

Both prophets had basically the same message: "God told you how you were supposed to live, how you were supposed to care for the vulnerable, and how you were supposed to fight for justice."

Jeremiah and Ezekiel, nationally and personally, were both in a difficult place like the prophets today. They both offer us great examples of living in times of similar work and simply a silent rivalry within our ranks.

The Luciferian spirit births silent rivalry among prophets. So how do we deal with it? Let me suggest four steps that you would be wise to employ as you grow and deal with this issue within your own life. When you're concerned that a silent rivalry is raging within your life, consider these 4 steps.

1. Prophet, know who you are, and if you do not, work on your personal self-esteem. Prophets with high anointings but fragile self-es-

teem are likely to be swallowed up in comparisons with other prophets whom they may covet.

2. Turn negative to positive by giving respect and showing love. Your brother and sister prophets want respect. They want to be seen, heard, validated, and accepted by the prophetic group, community, and spectrum.

Show them the example of how not to get sucked into competition, but show them support. Learn how to give your brother or sister prophet the proper acknowledgment they are due from you as a peer.

This will make it easier for them to open up and give the same to you in return. This also helps you see what the motivation is. Discern if it is one of competitiveness. When you encounter a prophetic brother or sister, and they have no interest in your achievements, take a step back and give the respect some time to settle itself.

3. As a prophet, you must know the difference between positive and negative forms of envy. Stop, learn, and know the difference between wanting something you can't have versus wanting something you can. Turn your envy into a motivation factor that can empower you and help you to grow and achieve. When you are unable to do this, then it is a negative waste of energy. Let me stress again. This is why the Luciferian spirit is so effective.

4. Confide in a mentor or confidant who you think might feel the same or might understand your feelings without judging. As prophets, we must learn how to speak our truth without blaming anyone and know why we want things to change and take responsibility. You must learn how to trust your leadership.

The Luciferian spirit is complex and the generational roots of this spirit have had a devastating effect on prophets. We can and we need to now discuss the issues of generational curses, the Luciferian spirit, and prophets.

CHAPTER 7

THE LUCIFERIAN SPIRIT, PROPHETS, AND GENERATIONAL CURSES

This issue is multifaceted and can be somewhat complex. When we think of the connection and the concept of generational curses and the influence of the "Luciferian spirit" on prophets, this is a serious issue. The very notion of curses transferred is sensitive to some and a way of life to others.

The idea of generational curses is often rooted in our beliefs and can be found in various cultural and spiritual contexts of our now day faith. This can vary from culture to culture. Prophets and generational curses are not new, as many times, we are the vehicles that God will use to uproot the spiritual bondage caused by curses.

Generation curses are a nice way of describing the bondage that has been passed down from one generation to another in the form of continual negative energy. This is the pattern of something being handed down from generation to generation. None of us are immune from this.

Generational curses are mainly the most prevalent attack of Satan upon prophets and the Luciferian spirit is the vehicle of the all-out war on the prophets. This is not to say others in the body of Christ are not under this attack also. This whole book is about prophets and the Luciferian spirit that prevails within our midst.

Understand that the Luciferian spirit wages war upon the prophets using a number of things like health problems, depression, alcoholism, or premature death just to name a few. The repeating of similar disorders and diseases from one generation to another is a commonly accepted phenomenon. There is a clear reason for this if we consider the spiritual effects of sin in the generational line. We also are to consider the issues I have already mentioned also.

Prophet, it is our genes that make us unique and our genes are affected as well as our spirits when we have generational curses in our life. Think about this, as the sins of the fathers now move forth to the third and fourth generations. A prophet can inherit the attributes or consequences of the sins that their predecessors committed generations ago.

This is why generational curses must be renounced. Notice Matthew Chapter One as Jesus did just that as He moved through 42 generations of his earthly family. Prophet, a close study of Matthew Chapter One will open eyes to generational curses and their effects.

The Luciferian spirit is the very thrust of fuel for the generational curse. The Luciferian spirit is a controlling general, an elite evil spirit who has the power to harass the descendants of a particular person who is prone to commit certain sins. Make no mistake about this demonic field general.

Within prophetic circles, we see the issue over and over with prophets: prophets who cannot find a prophetic home and the pattern of seeing them wander from prophetic group to prophetic group. This can also be from church to church or ministry to ministry. They become strangers within their own lands.

What's amazing is the pattern of doom that is seen almost everywhere they have been or they go to. Does this sound familiar? "No one wants me to prophesy" or "they did not want to let me speak." Again, they have become strangers, if it is only in their heads.

My all-time favorite is "they done me wrong," and this is true everywhere you have been. Amazing, simply so amazing. What are we not being told or what is it that we are missing?

This is a great concern as there are prophets who are living with an evil presence that has connected to their lives. This is what has generationally been passed to them and now the fight to identify it and disconnect from it is real. The struggle is massive and hard.

Can we look at the Luciferian spirit as the curse itself? We can believe that the curse is an actual evil spirit under the control of the Luciferian spirit. The reality is that the Luciferian Spirit and generational curses are distinct concepts connected by evil demonic order. The physical and spirit come together to ruin a life with purpose.

In this book and chapter, I am pointing out that the Luciferian spirit is the deployed field general of all evil, including the hereditary spirits that are referred to as demons. These spirits have been commonly connected to generational curses.

While we know that spiritual inheritance is the vehicle of choice for the "legal rights" of the devil. This is why our bodies, families, ministries, and churches are being attacked.

Do we really not think that the Luciferian spirit is not involved, I pray not. Again, I would like to point out that many leaders spend years and may never notice the Luciferian spirit, operating within their ministries. We can't continue to ignore this spirit and the damage it does.

This spirit is moving within its legal rights. Deliverance from these legal rights are broken through effective "prophetic insight," and anointed ministry, and prayer. Now, do you understand why the Luciferian spirit is so against prophets?

This is a job prophets that goes with the calling of the prophet. God has now a generation of prophets whom He has anointed to discern curses a person may possess birthed of the Luciferian spirit.

Generational curses can come from a multitude of places. This is where the Luciferian spirit may direct its attack from. Let's look at and list some of these places. My challenge to you is to find yourself on this list.

#1. Sin of our Ancestors: They are passed down through families. The sin has given the legal right to assault a prophet's body and finances because of what has happened in the past. We can't forget other issues like cancer, diabetes, seizures, mental illness, and what are described as incurable diseases that cause what seem like early deaths.

#2. Witchcraft: Some Prophets believe that they can be cursed by those who claim to have occult powers. The belief of the words of so called "witches" are looked upon as curses. They must be broken by the power of God. Do you or do you not believe the Word of God? Speak it upon yourself if this is an issue for you. Speak life to yourself prophet. You will not be able to help me or anyone else until you do. Become the first partaker.

#3. Prophet's Personal sins: Personal sin of a prophet that is connected to a forefather also committed those same sins. This could have been worship of other gods or any number of issues, where there is a legal vehicle to carry the curse from generation to generation.

Our nature is that we are creatures of habit and copy sinful behavior. We must realize that as prophets our being yoked to someone is the receipt of inheriting their problems too.

Deuteronomy 28:47-48 expounds on this very fact. We, the prophets of God, serve Him not with joyfulness and with gladness of heart, for the abundance of all things.

Yes, see the generational connection and the curse release as we serve our enemies. The curse of the enemy will attack us in hunger, thirst, and nakedness, and keep us in want of all things. We have to realize it and act upon it or it will destroy us.

We must be attentive to the influence of the Luciferian spirit in our lack. The prime effect of the Luciferian spirit of Poverty is not having what you need to do God's will. Prophets under this curse will squander, waste, and get into debt and bondage. We become prime candidates for get-rich schemes of all kinds.

Prophet, you must educate yourself if you have been cursed by your father's or your mother's lineage. Every prophet needs to see and have an understanding of generational curses and the influence of the Luciferian spirit. Have you ever wondered why some prophets hate prosperity with a passion? Go look at their backgrounds and the thinking becomes more understood as to why. This is just an example of why and how the generation curse works.

Ask yourself if curses are operating in your life. Ask God to identify the root. There are many different names we call curses in this day and time, many of which have seeped into our culture. It doesn't matter where you live in the world. There are curses that need to be broken that's through the bloodshed of Jesus.

As prophets especially if we simply act with our personal ungodly behavior similar to that of previous generations, we don't understand the reality of our salvation. Prophet, look at *Romans 10:9-10* and know that we are to confess as we speak that "Jesus is Lord," and believe in your heart that God raised Him and we will be saved." Prophet let's renew our minds.

Prophets, we must renew our minds and not forfeit the need for our accountability. Prophet, ensure that you renounce any wrongdoing, as curses are negated by our public confession of the devil and the Luciferian spirit combination.

We have to tell the enemy that "we cancel all demonic influence that may have been passed on to us from our ancestors. We must renounce all satanic assignments that have been directed toward our families and us in particular. Finally, we must reject all other possibilities whereby you may claim ownership of me." This is how we deal with the Luciferian spirit and the influence of generational curses. We confess that God's Love is stronger!

Scripturally, we must read and study *Leviticus 26:40-42*. Then we need to reference *Hosea 4:6* and pay close attention to the second part of the text. Prophet, when we reject God, His ways, and knowledge, we see that He will reject us and the sad part is that our children will suffer. This is too important to ignore.

Prophet, pray with me now. *"Heavenly Father, I stand right now in your courtroom to receive your righteous judgments over my bloodline inheritance right now. I renounce all the influence of the Luciferian spirit and all other demonic powers that have been attached to the bloodlines of my natural ancestors. God, I will respect and honor your righteous judgment over my genetic inheritance."*

This is so important to any prophet reading this. We all have to admit that we do have generational curses in our families. There is a cultural connection that we must not ignore, no matter where we are from. Once you do that know with all your heart that you are an overcomer, prophet.

This is why, Prophet, our attention now turns to prophetic breaches and the Luciferian spirit. The connection between the Luciferian spirit and prophetic breaches is reflected within the misuse of spiritual knowledge and power. Let's discuss this now and see why it's important.

CHAPTER 8

THE LUCIFERIAN SPIRIT AND PROPHETIC BREACHES

There is no doubt that much has been attached to the Luciferian spirit. To credit this spirit with the drama and evil it has caused is a total understatement. This is so true for the prophetic spectrum and ministry.

The word breach has multiple meanings, as a noun or a verb. To have a prophetic breach means breaking or failing to observe a covenant agreement or code of conduct as set by prophetic leaders or a prophetic overseer.

This could also mean the prophet's individual conduct within a prophetic operation fosters a gap or break in part or the whole overall operation of said operation.

Today many of us may also refer to this as a "falling out" with each other, as we see this a lot in the prophetic. When we "fall out," we don't talk, socialize, or have any communication. Most of the time we depend on others or social media to get information on what the other prophet or party is doing.

Let's now quickly review. The overall operations of our relationship have ceased. The reason is that we have a falling out or a breach in our relationship. This could be for a number of reasons. We all have or will experience this in some form or fashion. You're a prophet and you're having problems getting along with other prophets; consider these reasons why you may be having prophetic breaches in your life:

1. You know how you are upsetting other prophets but you don't care?
2. You don't know you are upsetting other prophets?
3. You are aware that you are upsetting other prophets but you don't quite understand why?

The Prophet Jeremiah helps us understand Prophetic Breaches. He became explicit in pointing out the social evils and injustice that prevailed, especially among the prophets of his era. Jeremiah warned them that the ruins of Shiloh served as an example of what would happen to Jerusalem *(Jeremiah 7:1-15)*. Many of his warnings and prophetic words were not taken seriously. Does that sound familiar?

Jeremiah's work as a prophet and the attitude of the other prophet's point to many parallels in this generation we see today! Let's start here to understand how the Luciferian spirit is working. The breaches are a legal spiritual pathway for the Luciferian spirit.

As we saw in the previous chapter of this book, this is similar to the move of this spirit generationally also. Again I ask you to read and study Matthew Chapter 1 and see the genealogy of Jesus and how he moved through his generational line to eradicate generational curses.

Here now, we see Jeremiah also boldly exposed the false teachings and corrupt practices of the religious leaders of his day, as Prophets of today should do. He called attention to unscriptural religious traditions and teachings, hypocritical actions, and religious exploitation and oppression. This is the Luciferian spirit moving forth against Jeremiah and moving today against us, the now-generation prophets.

Consequently, Jeremiah's ultimate perspective was that man's confidence in his wisdom, might, and riches were all futile. In light of this, it should be easy to see why Jeremiah did not get along with many prophets of his time.

He also did not have many relationships with anyone. Does that sound familiar? The relationships were pretty much nonexistent, as they clearly did not like or respect Jeremiah or his work for God.

Let's talk about today and why we see so many breaches in our prophetic relationships among prophets. This is why we have so many subcultures and counter-cultures among the prophetic ministry. The inner work of the Luciferian spirit in prophetic ministry can't be ignored.

We get mad because we can't get our way or we get offended and all of a sudden, we now become a prophetic work that is built on our unstable emotions, rather than God's foundation.

Let's talk about Prophetic Breaches courtesy of the Luciferian spirit. Here are 11 types of prophetic breaches that the Luciferian spirit causes within the prophetic community in this day and time. Division, destruction, and separation are the goals here.

1. The Prophet who is always threatened.

One of the reasons prophets don't honor each other is because they get threatened by each other. Sometimes prophets will get threatened by the way another prophet has a great rapport with another prophet or prophetic friend, and that prophet is threatened. Then of course how they may minister.

2. They become jealous very quickly.

Jealousy is a green-eyed demonic dragon that destroys love in any relationship. Prophets are this way until they mature. They can't help getting all worked up if your ministry is doing something they feel they should be doing and almost immediately, they become jealous. A jealous prophet is a prophet who does not know or understand their gift.

3. They can't tolerate your kind of prophet.

You may be in a group of prophets who have a charisma that puts you in high-profile places constantly and you're out of the group; peers just can't seem to like or get along with you. You will be that renegade prophet who always has something going on and they can't accept it or tolerate you in their midst.

4. The prophet who wants to be another prophet.

You're a prophet who may not have certain skills or gifts in other areas of the fivefold ministry, but you excel at administration within a prophetic operation.

You fit where you fit and many who see your work will never understand the price you paid to do what you do but they yearn to pull you down or embarrass you to get your so-called position. The saddest thing is most prophets never value what they already have and are too busy trying to be another prophet.

5. Prophets who love to hate you.

This prophet might not even know you, but if you are new in the ministry or church of fellowship, this type of prophet becomes absolutely judgmental about you simply because they don't know you.

Everything concerning you is always expressed negatively, of course until they need you. This type of prophet will love to hate you with the other prophets who are not in their immediate social circle.

6. The prophet who is used to being the center of attraction.

An immature prophet can't share the anointing of God upon someone other than them. Many of them used to be the center stage and once God uses another prophet, they now have a problem, and hate them immediately.

Sometimes, God will use a prophet out of the norm for a task that someone else may do on a regular basis, and from that moment on that prophet is hated with a passion.

7. The prophet who can't stand up to issues.

This type of prophet likes to sugarcoat issues and does not like to confront issues. This type of prophet does not like a prophet who is straight up or speaks their mind respectfully even in disagreement. The prophet who can't stand up to issues will have issues with you! Because you talk a different language from them, you are direct and to the point and they are not. This type of prophet will have problems with you and others who are direct.

8. The prophet who is always competitive.

This type of prophet is constantly comparing everything from your dress to your offering to your ministry schedule. Even for trivial things that you may do differently, they are secretly in competition with you, and even if they masquerade as your friend, understand they do not like you.

This is the classic Friend-A-Me Prophet and they are a dangerous person in your life until you fully identify them. The sooner you do, the better off you will be. Ensure yourself that you are fair in your judgment.

9. The self-conscious prophet.

Some prophets are self-conscious about everything that they have. From the money they are making to ministry connections to clothes and people they know who you do not know, this type of prophet seems to be at a constant war with their inner self.

Some prophets know how to use this to get better each day while other Prophets use self-consciousness to compare with other prophets and yes they harbor an inner hate because they are self-conscious.

10. The prophet who is addicted to gossiping.

Immature prophets, no matter how gifted they are, will gossip and have an everlasting bond, to gossip until they grow out of it and mature. This type of prophet loves gossiping about everything and everybody, especially other prophets, about their business, their walk with God, and how they handled difficult situations.

Remember, this type of prophet will always discuss your business and whatever you confided with them with someone else., namely another gossiping prophet.

11. The prophet who has to protect what's theirs.

It takes time for prophets to become real friends, especially mature prophets. It just does not happen, and most prophets have a list of people they trust on one hand and still have some fingers left.

Fear of encroachment by another prophet in their space without it being earned is and most likely will be viewed with resentment and hatred. When prophets do not know how to respect others who have a like or similar gift, there will be conflict.

Did you see yourself in any of these 11 prophetic breaches? Prophetic sibling conflict occurs because we're selfish by nature. It's natural for some prophets to have a hard time getting along. Prophetic conflict can also be caused by foolishness and anger.

Within the prophetic ranks, we need to understand that selfishness will always manifest itself as wanting to be first and having the best. The issue is deeper than we may totally understand as we become increasingly aware of the Luciferian spirit.

The Luciferian spirit has represented itself in different forms throughout history. Sometimes as a philosophical and spiritual movement, it encompasses the search for enlightenment, knowledge, and personal freedom as it seeks to use and destroy us.

Throughout the scriptures, we see the prophets raised up in unity, working together in companies or schools for the purposes of God. Yes, we see the Luciferian spirit work to advocate for the liberation of the perceived constraints, whether societal, religious, or moral. The Luciferian spirit is a destroyer in all sense of the word.

What is sad is that today, many use the Luciferian spirit as only a metaphorical representation of satan and do not understand the potential of what happens within the prophetic groups and lives of prophetic individuals under this attack.

So many factors of special insight we are hit with today, from many individuals to groups who want to affect trends and ways within the body of Christ. This is a fact and yes let's be sure. The prophets, seers, watchmen, or even visionaries have been given the assignment to bridge the gap between the earthly and the divine. We are conveying messages or warnings to humanity. This is our job. This has been our job throughout history.

Our problem occurs when numerous figures have emerged, claiming divine revelation and prophetic insights, shaping the course of civilizations and religious beliefs. Let's go back again to chapter one of this book and see the work of the Luciferian spirit starting.

The advent of social media and technology has, in reality, solidified the connection between the Luciferian spirit and prophetic breaches as we see multiple examples of potential misuse or misinterpretation of spiritual knowledge and power.

There is no doubt that some prophets have been led astray, blurring the line between genuine spiritual insight and self-serving manipulation.

The Luciferian spirit actually will seduce some prophets who seek power and control over others. The very influence of the Luciferian spirit forces prophetic breaches for personal gain or to manipulate the masses.

History has shown this very fact. Apostle Paul faced some difficult problems, including disunity among the believers. First Corinthians 13, the chapter of love, was written for the prophetic people at Corinth to get along. We, the now generation prophets, should adopt it.

Too many prophetic ministries have blown up in the past for the lack of love. Do me a favor. Go back and read this paragraph again and then reflect on your experiences. This is not to make you feel bad but to point out that so many of us have dealt with this process or we are dealing with this process.

The prophetic without love is "noise" and "nothing." *(I Corinthians 13)* Many in the body of Christ are simply too quick to dismiss the prophetic because they believe it is too divisive and they don't trust what they do not understand. Prophets we must be educated so we can educate others as we demonstrate, display Godly behavior, and fulfill God's agenda and purpose.

Unfortunately, for so many in the prophetic community, we have no real working relationships with those outside our sphere of influence. This is true and can be said for many of our peer prophets of today. The reality is that it is hard for us to get along.

That is an understatement. We have developed, graced, and organized ourselves by our ambition and not by our work. This is the work of the Luciferian spirit as it comes into focus here as it wants us to skip, take shortcuts, and hate on our peer prophets.

Some of you may choose to ignore this issue, but I am not led to. The struggle has been too hard and the cost too high for this writer, to ignore yet another divisive issue in the body of Christ, especially among the seers.

Have you ever wondered why prophets don't seem to get along with themselves and people in general, especially in the Body of Christ? The reasons can be almost endless. They can range from mentality, spirituality, lineages, cultures, norms, and even race. Yes, all these things in the quote on quote, Body of Christ. The Seers of God.

Simply consider how critical we can be of each other and other prophetic leaders. Prophets too often believe they know what is right and wrong just because they have the title. We are not all-knowing. God is all-knowing.

A critical word has to be given without hurting people but maintain the integrity of the prophetic as you speak in love, or we will open yet another breach.

Can you see us prophet, as we live like this? We are candidates for frustration at every turn. Frustration is a useful tool of the Luciferian spirit. Prophets, we must learn to live with and overcome frustration, as it will surely show up in our lives to create prophetic breaches.

We define frustration prophetically as when nothing happens or things get worse for the recipient after you give a prophetic word. Also, we probably need to consider when others question your theology due to your prophetic gifting.

Then there is listening to strong prophetic people who are telling you multiple different things that are contrary things to do. One thing is for sure, it will show up in different ways for different prophets.

Not only do you feel frustration but rejection. Sometimes, your prophetic words may be rejected and criticized by others. The Old Testament prophets often were rejected. Rejection is a common experience for people in prophetic ministry. Prophet, I am saying you will learn to live and deal with breaches, but it should not stop us from striving to learn from and empower each other.

Prophetic breaches and the characteristics we describe are real out-front enemies of prophetic ministry. Prophet, if you do not master your frustration, you will never develop.

This enemy, the hidden Luciferian spirit, will always infect the word we have, and give an unevenly yoked perspective on your life, ministry, and work prophet. This includes abroad and in the church or ministry.

The one thing we must remember is that our prophetic gift is not more important than the purposes of God within the Body of Christ. This is how we combat the Luciferian spirit. We keep the main thing the main thing and we don't fall into pride, and temptation and pro-claim and act superior to others.

Let's be serious. There is a huge silence on this subject of the Prophet and the Luciferian spirit. This silence by the church gives the opportunity for others to define prophets as new age, quacks, false, or demonic. Many modern-day prophets are seen as having zero to no credibility and automatically labeled a "false" prophet.

The point here is that the ability of the Luciferian spirit is vast. The very topic of prophetic breaches hides the unseen force of the Luciferian spirit.

Is it any wonder when people start to move in the prophetic min-istry that the church automatically casts suspicion? Some prophets and prophetic people in established churches have to operate under the radar or keep quiet so at least other Christians won't label them in negative terms.

In many churches, prophetic people are not supported or empowered but often are tolerated and criticized. Sadly, too many prophetic people either leave their churches or if they constantly feel minimized and unfulfilled in their gifts. Does this sound like you?

Can you see the absolute refined work of the Luciferian spirit? How it works behind the scenes to create prophetic breaches that are designed to keep us apart and never establish unity.

They, the emerging and young prophets, now develop a "persecution complex" or slink off wallowing in self-pity like rebellious Absalom, subtly speaking words against the leadership and growing my own reputation thereby.

Rebellion can greatly affect the words we bring to leaders, and yet many prophets seem to hardly know they have a problem in this area. If you can't sit under authority today, you will be a pain in the neck to tomorrow's leaders too. Deal with your rebellion now, or miss out. It's that simple.

We now will address another critical issue in the person of the issue of roaming "lone ranger prophets and how the Luciferian spirit affects them.

The key issue here is dealing with the Dead Wisdom of the Luciferian Prophet. In Chapter Nine, we will explore this topic as there are prophets who need to be aware of this issue. There is much to discuss, so let's grab some tea and keep reading.

CHAPTER 9

THE LUCIFERIAN SPIRIT VERSES THE DEAD WISDOM OF A PROPHET

Scripture tells us that the word of a wise man's mouth is gracious. A fool's lips will swallow him up. Using this reference in *Ecclesiastes 10:12*, let us not forget that gracious words are those filled with gestures of unearned kindness. Do you know how to talk to other prophets, your brothers and sisters in Christ, or even the worldly people?

The wise prophet, who wants to develop good relationships, looks for good and complementary things to sow into others. They understand the communication process. Everyone wants to be around those who are gracious with their speech and not a fool.

Think now of the roaming prophet, who is trying to fit in. They may come from another area or simply another group. Leaders, this is why you must know of and recognize the Luciferian spirit characteristics. This spirit is masked up so often in the undisciplined issues of prophets.

There are always valid reasons why a prophet may roam to find a prophetic home. Then there are reasons why prophets roam and they can find peace unless they are peace breakers of the existing peace. Sounds funny but it is true.

Proverbs 16:7 tells us that when our ways please God, even our enemies will be at peace with us. This is especially true of the prophetic.

Roaming Prophets are defined in many ways. This can depend on the prophetic leader whom you ask. Most often, we see them as prophets looking to connect because of something that happened somewhere else. This is why they roam, to get away from a situation they have no desire for.

Let me be clear again. There are always valid reasons why a prophet may be roaming, looking for fellowship. We will not disrespect that fact. I and many others know what it is like to be roaming and looking for fellowship and leadership.

Let's, for conversation's sake, identify this prophet as associated with rebellion, unnatural enlightenment, and the pursuit of forbidden knowledge to the extent of even being called out for witchcraft. This is a real reality; if you talk to some established prophetic leaders, many will share some aspects of this concept.

These are some of the very same things we see the Luciferian spirit identified with. Furthermore, as we explore the connection between this enigmatic spirit and the dead wisdom of a prophet, we are seeking to unravel an intricate web of deception that binds them together.

The Luciferian spirit, as it affects roaming prophets, represents a profound desire for personal freedom, autonomy, and even self-reflection to shine at the direct expense of others.

Some roaming prophets are just that, full-time roamers because they challenged established mandatory principles and training and the wisdom of prophetic authorities whom God has in position. They simply do not want to deal with the process of development many prophetic leaders speak about.

The Luciferian spirit in the life of this prophet has captured the courage of a prophet to confront society and its issues. Now we see their ways are not the ways not of God. This spirit will consistently be connected with things like talking to the dead, and a pursuit of knowledge, mainly into forbidden territories like witchcraft to make them have favor.

Prophets, throughout history, have served as conduits for divine wisdom and revelation from God. Their role is to transmit messages from a higher power to guide and enlighten humanity. This is what we do.

The wisdom prophets impart often transcends the boundaries of time, resonating with generations to come. As a noun, we see wisdom as the quality of having experience, knowledge, and good judgment.

Wisdom connects with words such as intelligence, understanding, good sense, common sense, prudence, and logic, just to name a few. Wisdom is the validation of a decision or action. It is the glue of experience, judgment, and knowledge in the Body of Christ. We see wisdom in the body of knowledge and principles that develop within a specified society, such as the Body of Christ. Our wisdom comes and originates from the word of God.

The Wisdom of God is the word of God. There is life in the word of God, which means there is life in the wisdom of God. The wisdom of God is the greatest goal in any situation and the best way to achieve that goal. God's wisdom always sees the big picture in focus. Wisdom is different from knowledge.

The Luciferian spirit, as you should see by now, wants to kill our wisdom. Unfortunately, we have a lot of our prophetic peers without wisdom. They are overwhelmed and yet they are brilliant but have no wisdom. Without Godly wisdom, we are without knowledge. To know and understand the best way to achieve a goal, you have to be able to integrate the factors from various sources of knowledge and experience.

Psalm 147:5 says, "His understanding simply has no end." *Daniel 2:21-22* says, "God changes the times and seasons; God will remove kings and establish kings." God will deal with leaders. The wisdom of God is the knowledge to those who have an understanding of His ways, as God reveals the deep and hidden things.

Dead wisdom in the life of a prophet is birthed in the counsel of the ungodly that we take for being Godly. Who are you listening to prophet?

Dead wisdom is birthed again in the counsel of the ungodly. That prophet would rather live by it and be accepted than hurt, be alone, and allow the presence of God to continue the developmental process. This is not a sold-out to God prophet.

See the Luciferian spirit's shadow upon this type of prophet. Many are true enough roaming prophets, who are going from place to place because they are looking to be connected. They have been hurt, violated, and mentally destroyed by the Luciferian spirit. They have not healed and that is why the prophetic leader must know something about the Luciferian spirit.

The life of that prophet keeps them in what we call simply a rut. Have you ever been stuck in a certain place in life that makes you bitter and not better? You were living by a set of guidelines that are working against you. You just keep doing it as you see everyone as your enemy, especially leadership. This is why there is a seeking to change leadership all the time.

For a prophet, we should experience wisdom daily that's elevated in God's word with revelation. Let's look at Psalms 1 as we see examples of wisdom that is unfruitful or simply dead wisdom.

Prophet, the word says, "Blessed as you walk not in the counsel of the ungodly, nor do you establish your way as that of sinners." Prophet, if you're going to be blessed, you must walk not in the wisdom or counsel of this world, but in the counsel of God's ways or God's operations.

As prophets, we must get rid of any wisdom that is blocking our blessings. This is dead wisdom. This is what the Luciferian spirit desires to do to your life.

Some dead wisdom, as we all have been connected to is selfishness, prejudice, and hatred of certain types of people of a nationality. How much wisdom have you been exposed to that relates to denominations and genders that are blocking your blessings? These are fair questions that need to be answered by you and me in a self-examination.

This is the counsel of the ungodly. The Luciferian spirit has us doing things in a certain way that we know have not been fruitful and are not of God. How much inner prejudice are we still holding on to that is blocking our blessings? Answer the question, prophet.

Ungodly counsel will always produce dead wisdom. This is true whether you are a roaming prophet or an established prophet. The example of prophetic men and women mistreating each other and the body of Christ as a whole is a classic example.

Let's look at the individual prophetic level as we see the issues of dead wisdom in the lives of prophets. Issues like domestic violence, child abuse, drug abuse, sex abuse, and being carriers of gossip and filled with pride are just some examples of being under ungodly counsel.

Prophets, have we determined who and who should not counsel us by our pride and being just plain stubborn? Dead wisdom and ungodly counsel have and will continue to destroy prophets and prophetic ministries.

How many times have we seen prophets ascending in ministry and then becoming the victim of ungodly counsel by someone who was scorned? Someone who was secretly jealous, or our inflated sense of self-counsel as we compare and contrast ourselves to others.

How many times have we seen or experienced someone who was scorned and passed it on to a prophet? Now that prophet is hurt, wounded even more and they fail to develop because someone in their life who they valued has been scorned. That person passes on ungodly counsel to them that manifests in dead wisdom.

They key to being blessed is to catch the vision of your leadership. This is a reason why a prophet may be roaming and looking and hurt because they are connected with some dead wisdom. Prophets if you need to ask a question about your leadership, then ask. Stop assuming when you don't know.

If you don't know the vision, then ask, and keep asking until you understand the vision. A prophet cannot serve effectively under any mantle that does not have the proper level of wisdom. The fact is true.

Look around. How many prophets do we know who are serving, but they are lost? Someone is telling them they are anointed, appointed of God and that same person or person is not requiring a standard for that prophet's life, nor will they adhere to a standard. We are hurting the prophetic community and enhancing the Luciferian influence.

We all should be upset to see our prophetic peers more concerned with being seen than developing. Why does the prophet of today feel no need to learn basic church functions and no need to register and maintain a legal ministry in their state of record? Also, who has made us, the prophets, exempt from giving to God?

This influence of dead wisdom is destroying the prophetic and it is up to us as leaders to correct this grave error. Allow me to ask the question. Who has coached us? Who has mentored us to the point that we are willing to walk through the body of Christ and exercise dead wisdom and think it is perfectly ok? I ask again, who?

Some of our now-generation prophets and seers need to awaken to this as we are bringing curses upon ourselves. Some who read this will no doubt be offended, but I reach out to you to understand if you love the prophetic ministry as I do, and you have been given the opportunity to have this as your platform and life's work, then yes there is relevance proof for this subject to be raised.

When will we prioritize the word of God and become a clear example, not a cluttered ungodly example of the word of God? This is a task that requires our attention more than a lot of us are willing to give.

Think about it, and then let's look at ourselves as prophets. The word is going to be everything to us. It will be our friend, doctor, lawyer, and whatever it needs to be to direct us. Without the Word, we have dead wisdom because we allow ungodly counsel to dominate and direct our lives.

This is how you can examine the Luciferian spirit in the life of a prophet. Again, it can be a roaming prophet, a lone ranger prophet, or a prophet in general.

The word of God keeps a prophet's personal life in perspective. It keeps the prophet grounded, hungry, and humble. It keeps the prophet focused, willing, and able to do the work of God.

Someone sitting in the seat of the scornful will always deliver counsel and perspective that has been tainted with personal ungodly counsel. The real word of God will have us planted by the rivers of life as they move. We will not move because we are stable.

When our peers or our haters deal with us, can they see and sense that we, the prophets of God, are stable like a tree? Who can count on us because we are stable? Can your apostle count on you? Can your brother or sister prophet count on you?

Are you positioned under an apostle or in a church? Can the local pastor count on you if they need to prophet? Rest assured prophets who walk in dead wisdom are not stable. They are wishy-washy. This is why we have so many prophets wanting to be blessed and elevated.

This type of prophet does not understand the covenant and will not honor covenant and will turn on you because the dead wisdom they operate in has only one rule. That rule is me, myself, and I as I will cut, backstab and most of all, smile in your face as I stab you in the back. My loyalty is to myself.

Dead wisdom makes this type of prophet feel they have a right to assume this type of action. You cannot be friends with this type of prophet. It is literally impossible while the prophet operates in dead wisdom. Understand this fact. Let me say again that the influence of the Luciferian spirit is real, not imagined.

Question? Can your kids, wife, or husband count on you to be stable? Are you the prophetic tree example in your city, state, country, ministry, or church? Are you the one that everyone knows where you stand in God?

Can you answer those questions and establish the fact that you're aware and free of the Luciferian influence? Are you the source of consistent blessings or the consistent curse to everything and everyone you encounter?

Repeat this, "As I come into my new season, I will have consistent blessings, not just an every now and then blessings, but my blessings will be consistent because I will not operate in dead wisdom. I will operate in the will of God. In the name of Jesus, God I give you all the Glory!"

Now shout "Glory" because you now know that the moment you act like a tree and exercise stability, you will then become a candidate for consistent blessings. The stable prophet of God is operating in this type of anointing and the standard is nothing less.

Throughout this book, my goal has been to equip you with a deeper and more profound now day insight of the Luciferian spirit. I have painted a picture of the Luciferian spirit operating as a shadow presence in all of the previous chapters.

Now it is time for us to see the Luciferian's presence copy the shadow anointing of God. We need to discuss this as we compare the shadow presence of the Luciferian Spirit versus The Shadow Anointing. Let's do that right now, as there is a serious connection.

CHAPTER 10

THE LUCIFERIAN SHADOW VERSUS THE SHADOW ANOINTING

The very concept of "shadow" often refers to the power of God. There have been different things, like oil in the Old Testament, that are seen as a representation of God's power. This also is a representation of God's power.

Probably the most famous concept of the shadow anointing is the account of Peter's shadow in *Acts 5:15*. This is the place where people who were sick were healed and even people who had been laid out on the streets were healed. This is all because of the Shadow of Peter.

This is about the shadow anointing, which is deeply connected to the practice of healing and represents the spirit of God. Lucifer is the ultimate counterfeit, as we have seen his Luciferian spirit run wild within the prophetic circles. This spirit has played cat and mouse and yes it has operated as a shadow.

Over the years, we have blamed many different types of spirits and have we really understood the multiple manifestations of the Luciferian spirit and how it has manipulated us through lesser manifestations? The point is that we have not recognized this spirit and now we must.

There is a connection here that I want you to see with the Luciferian spirit and how it has copied and attempted to destroy the prophetic ministry. The concept of the shadow anointing is also associated with the biblical account of Peter's shadow; this is where we see the sick laid in streets so the shadow of Peter may fall on them for healing. We must look closer here.

The shadow anointing is deeply intertwined with Peter. Those of different faiths will also have different interpretations of the shadow anointing. I clearly will not debate that, and that is why Peter is my subject of comparison as to how the Shadow of the Luciferian spirit affects us.

Let's do some history with Peter. Look at *Acts 3:6-8*. A man, "lame from his mother's womb," asked alms of them as they passed. What was apparent was that everyone passed him by but not Peter and John. Finding a new level of faith, Peter said deliberately and clearly: *"Silver and gold, I do not have. I will give you what I have. Now receive in the name of Jesus. Now get up and walk."* We all know the story.

God's power was demonstrated as the lame man was healed. Peter, who we know was one of the original 12 apostles, didn't forget that fact. His confidence rose. He was a recipient of a deposited experience. He would later become the leader of the apostles, after Jesus' ascension. There is a plan in place for his life here.

Look at the church at this time; as its apostle, prophet, and seer, Peter grew and became a real leader. He led the church into fulfilling the commission of Jesus. The commission that was to go ye into all the world. The assignment is to preach the gospel to everyone. Peter is a prophet of change. There is no doubt. While some may major on his faults, I relate to his rise as a leader and exponent of God's purposes.

As a prophet, you can expect God's power to be demonstrated through you as we see in the example of Peter. Over and over, as God used Peter, we see him staying humble and understanding who he was. This is a key here.

He did this despite the assumptions people had of John and himself. Many people felt they had special powers. He had to let them know it was God and not him.

People wanted to believe there was something special about Peter. Peter is operating at a high level of the anointing at this stage in his life. This is a fact. The reality that this is dangerous for immature prophets is an understatement.

They began seeking his company and a relationship with him, hoping to have some power pass over them. Does this sound familiar to you as we look at prophets today? Here come prophets with the wrong motives and focus. This happens more often than we care to admit.

Just imagine people carrying the sick out into the streets and laying them on cots and pallets. They now wait for Peter to come by. His shadow might fall on any one of them. Wow, the thought of this is mind-blowing. This is real power. Look how Peter handles this as we keep looking at the events of the Shadow anointing.

Look at the people from the cities in the vicinity of Jerusalem. People who were traveling together to come. People being unified for a common cause. Here, we see people who were sick, afflicted, and dealing with unclean spirits, and they were all being healed. This is amazing. What is so special that people believed in what Peter had, but Peter did not acknowledge himself in the manner they did?

During this time, we notice that healings and miracles are taking place through the apostles and prophets. We see that the anointing was so profound and powerful on Peter that even his shadow was enough to bring transformation in *Acts 5*.

Let's notice that Apostle Peter's shadow is falling on people. Crowds gathered and the sick and those who had evil spirits were healed. All of them as the word of God tells us. What exactly are we talking about? Glad you asked.

How was the shadow anointing birthed, and why? The word "shadow" means covering. This was a covering for Peter. Who was his covering? The Lord. The Holy Spirit.

Peter is walking in an anointing that all prophets need and that's revelation of who he is. He is a servant and revelation is our prophetic life force. It means again, "a Covering." Prophet, can you be a steward for this type of covering?

People had high regard for Peter's miracle-working ability despite the fact he told them it was God and not him. Sounds like people today as they placed faith in the efficacy of Peter's shadow. Just like today, people are attracted to the gift, not the person. They want the gift. To add to the fact that all were healed, even those who were not under his shadow. How do we explain this for those who were not under Peter's shadow?

Prophets, listen closely. To simply trust a shadow is clearly not wise. What if it had been a cloudy day at high noon? Imagine if that day Peter had no shadow at all to speak of.

We must understand that God's power to heal is not dependent on anything but God. No one has to be in the right place, at the right time, under the right conditions. Shadows come and go, but God's power is constant. This is what the Luciferian spirit can't duplicate. Remember this point.

The shadow of Peter was his actual carrying of the Glory of God. Check and see, your shadow may go about 4-6 feet in one direction. There is no way you can minister to several thousand people with that size shadow but when the glory is upon you, you can.

You would simply give out from the walking back and forth. Do you see why the Luciferian spirit tries to duplicate the Holy Spirit and it can't? Prophet there is a major difference between operating in the shadows and having a shadow of God upon you.

This is simply why prophets who operate under this shadow are different than those who choose to operate out of the will of God. My prayer is that you will see this fact and adopt it.

How do we get this shadow, which is really the overshadowing of the presence of God, the Shekinah glory of God that hovers over us? We can get the presence of God to tangibly hover over us and anybody who comes near it will receive its effects. How obedient and dedicated are we prophets?

Exodus 13:21 presents us with an example of this concept. The LORD went before the people during the day. He was in a pillar of a cloud. He leads them at night in a pillar of fire. This was their source and the guidance they needed to give them light to travel with day or night.

Consider now that because of God's overshadowing presence on Peter, he didn't even touch the people. The Lord did it by His shadow. This was his guidance. The overshadowing presence of God can recreate organs of the body that don't even exist. When a prophet gets the shadow upon their life, people's lives are changed wherever they are or go.

Here are some prophetic keys we must consider now as we talk about the shadow anointing. Let's now compare it to what the Luciferian spirit will do to the prophet. This is critically important as we understand what the Luciferian does as it shadows us.

Jesus taught and trained Peter daily. He walked with him in the hills outside. He spent precious time with him in Capernaum. He sat with him beside the sea they both loved so much. Jesus stayed in Peter's home, ate at his table, and gave blessings to his family and friends. The point here is that Peter was coachable, trainable, and humble and he had a relationship with Jesus.

Let's relate this to the point that Peter was not a know it all, who wanted a title and you could not tell him anything. We see and have established that the Luciferian spirit will not allow a prophet to be properly mentored in this manner. Think how Peter watched in silence as Jesus, time after time, cast out devils, healed the sick, and restored the blind. The point here is that He allowed himself the opportunity to learn.

The Luciferian spirit will want to do this itself and not learn. This spirit will have a prophet thinking they are ready to do something they may have never done, only watched. This spirit will disrespect the process of mentorship over and over.

The fact was that Jesus called his disciples together, chose 12 from among them to be apostles, and ordained Peter to be the president of the council they now constituted was special. This newly appointed apostle and prophet watched, learned, and added to his faith, wholly absorbed in the life of his teacher. The point here is that Peter did not ignore instruction but became a student of his craft. Peter embraced his mentorship. Prophets who submit to the Luciferian spirit will not embrace mentorship. They will ignore it. Becoming a student of the prophetic is needed and necessary when you have an opportunity like Peter did. The greatest level of respect is that you become a student of your craft.

Over and over, Peter eagerly walked along the path of miracle after miracle as he traveled with Jesus. Scripture tells us how he stood in wonder as the Redeemer took the lifeless hand of a child and commanded her to arise.

Luke 8 details that Peter had never witnessed such an event as "her spirit came again, and she arose straightway." Peter pondered these things in his heart. The deposited experience is critical. He did not know that he would have a similar moment in *Acts 9:40,* taking another beloved woman by the hand to raise her from the dead. He did not try to duplicate or move too fast. He studied, learned, and put the work in. He allowed himself to be covered fully with God's shadow.

This is what the Luciferian spirit will not allow in the prophetic. True to form, it wants to take God's place in your life. This spirit does shadow the prophet in a totally opposite manner than the Spirit of God does. Prophets who choose to move before their time is seemly a most common, almost daily issue. Even now in this day and time, we are still dealing with this issue.

Peter's faith began to reach heights virtually unequaled as Peter is the only person in the New Testament to ever walk on water. This act of faith has never been recorded of any other mortal man. Yes, we see his faith faltered because of treacherous waves and adverse winds. So before we judge him, what can we learn from him?

As a follower of Jesus and an apostle and prophet, Peter was more than show. He had substance and was the real deal for Jesus. We need more Peters in the prophetic community who are willing to give God their all.

This is why we have to see ourselves, who are we? Peter had his faults but he never stopped learning. The Luciferian spirit will have us elevating ourselves to where we have not been prepared for.

Funny how our self-gratification gives us such a sense of an inflated ego and opinion of ourselves. The prophetic is a breeding ground for this.

Peter still had many lessons to learn in the days ahead. He learned in the kingdom of God that no man's strength is sufficient. The Luciferian spirit aims to make you feel different.

The sobering, sorrowing realization that he was not of himself made him capable of what God requires was perhaps the final ingredient in Peter's personal preparation. This is exactly what the Luciferian spirit wants us to think and embrace of it.

No one, nothing can harm you if you have the shadow of God upon your life. The shadow is the Holy Ghost, the Spirit of God. It will overshadow, protect, and provide for you. It will release healing.

He will release blessings to you and to everybody you meet. There will be people radically changed and all you do is walk past them or happen to be in the same building.

Do you want the shadow anointing in your life? Matthew 6:6 says for us to enter into thy place of prayer and pray to thy Father in secret. Spend time with the Father who sees in secret shall reward you openly.

God rewards us with His presence. This is what every prophet should want. In *Genesis 15:1,* God says, "I am thy shield, and thy exceeding great reward."

Prophet, there is no greater reward that God can give you than to give you Himself. He is the source of wealth and life prosperity. God wants to bless prophets and seers with the ability to acquire, create, and maintain wealth.

That means divine favor wherever you go. The shadow causes you to get what others can't get. It causes you to be able to do what others can't do. It causes you to have results that others can't have.

Notice that in the body of Christ, people always seem to point out certain things about Apostle Peter, denouncing his character, lack of humility, fear of man, and failure to pray. Prophets, you should know how people say things about us as prophets. This is what they do. They won't stop unfortunately.

You can't help share and develop prophets of relevance unless you are relevant yourself. This Peter was not the Peter who was a diamond that had to be cut, trimmed, corrected, and then polished. He was a diamond who needed and did the necessary work.

This is us today. Peter gave us the example of not skipping the process. Peter was a prophet who grew and matured. He was someone Jesus knew he could trust to receive the keys of the kingdom. He was tested so he could be trusted.

The Luciferian spirit cast upon a prophet will change that prophet. The conduct we see of Peter will be the absolute opposite of a prophet under this spirit.

Peter is a shining example of what God looks for in a prophet, especially in the way of character and substance. The seducing of the Luciferian spirit elevates a prophet's self-opinion of himself.

The prophet becomes unteachable, untrainable, and a threat to the Prophetic community as an enemy within. We must learn how to identify the Luciferian spirit and destroy it from within our ranks. Prophets inform the Luciferian spirit that it is no longer or not welcome in your life, circles, or ministry.

Finally, I would like to share what I believe are safety rules for protecting Prophets, Seers, Watchman and Apostles. These rules are meant for those who are serious about this walk. Join me and others as we move forth. We have not arrived; we all have work to do. Let me say that again. We all have work to do.

CHAPTER 11

THE PROPHET'S SAFETY RULES FOR THE LUCIFERIAN SPIRIT

Throughout history, we have seen accidents and strange things happen in people's lives, including prophets. The secular field has employed occupational accident prevention. Where do you think it came from? This is just one of the many things the world has taken from God's Word and used.

Safety rules were developed for worker safety. The prophet's safety rules are to be employed because of the nature of the prophet's calling. The Luciferian spirit wants to control the prophetic gift for its own work and bidding.

The following basic safety rules are worth knowing. Here are ten basic safety rules for any type of profession. Stay with me here. Soon, you will see the point.

1. Understand where you're at. Know your surroundings because a worker is less likely to get hurt if they know where they are and what's around them.
2. Make sure your garments are appropriate and correct.
3. Know the tools of your craft and understand the art of it.

4. Know how to employ your craft and honor it by being a student.
5. Understand that your work is work. You are there for a reason.
6. Strive to be clean. Good housekeeping reduces hazards.
7. Keep communication channels open. Always report accidents and issues of defective equipment and or unsafe conditions.
8. Use first aid even if it seems to be of no significance or minor. Your personal neglect may lead to serious incidents.
9. Be proactive with safety. Share an idea if you feel it will reduce accidents. Tell your supervisor about it.
10. Do not take unnecessary chances. Next to sheer carelessness, shortcuts are probably the biggest killer of all.

These are 10 basic safety rules for any job. They sure sound a lot like the prophetic and how we develop. What happens if your job is to be a mouthpiece of God?

You have been chosen and now how do we employ as prophets' safety rules for prophets? What are the rules that will allow us to be effective and not be a prophetic accident and lead ourselves to prophetic suicide? The first and constant thing we should do is pray.

We should always engage in prayer, especially when we are under attack. This is a prayer to say when you know you are under attack by Satan or the Luciferian spirit.

Say this prayer and believe that you will be freed from this attack. This prayer breaks satan's demonic communications with the demons of his kingdom and gives you the victory! Read this prayer over and over until you commit it to memory.

The Prophet's Safety Prayer

Father, in the Name of Jesus, your servant is under attack! Principalities have received an assignment against me, and now powers are active in their motions against me. Right now, God, I pray for this demonic assignment on me to be broken in the name of Jesus.

Communications and motions of both principalities and powers stop now and be confused in the name of Jesus. Lying vanities and wiles right now, you are rendered Inactive! I decree and declare no more communication with satan, the Luciferian spirit, or any demonic manifestation. I submit myself totally unto God.

I speak total resistance to you satan. My words, thoughts, and deeds are no longer influenced by demonic motives. I'm in God's complete safety. I am totally protected. Thank you Jesus. The power of God has freed me totally. I am free in Jesus' name. Amen!

Prophet, you must always establish these prophetic safety rules in your life. This is how we break the stronghold of the Luciferian spirit within our lives and within the prophetic community.

1. You always want satan to know you are not confused. Prophet, the first place satan attacks is your mind. Why? If he can mess up your mind, he can make you follow him instead of God.

First, satan will try to blank out your mind so that you will not even think about God. Here, we have the influence of the Luciferian spirit and how it affects your life and relationships with your leaders.

Mark 4:2-25 tells the parable of the seeds where satan comes and takes away the seed, which is the Word of God. Satan has started so many false beliefs, doctrines, and people who call themselves prophets who are not.

This work of satan is meant to lead you away from the true Word of God. Prophets, please understand that satan leads you to jump to this religion or cult and fills your mind so full of false ideas that you no longer are able to distinguish the truth.

The Luciferian spirit will have prophets agree with the latest spiritual fad. Only by turning to Jesus Christ, crying out to Jesus for truth, will you be able to break away from this demonic hold. You are the mouthpiece of God; you can't afford confusion.

2.You always want satan to know you understand his demonic structure. Prophet, when you don't understand the structure, you will lend a foothold to the devil. *Ephesians 4:27* tells us to give the devil no foothold. So what is a foothold in our lives?

A foothold is anything that will give the devil access to affect our lives. There are innumerable ways the devil affects our lives and all of these things can be classified into four different categories:

1. Generational Curses
2.Sins that we, as prophets, will commit
3.Sins committed against us
4.Trauma and accidents.

Think of how the devil wants to affect us through these options.

3.You always want satan to know you know that you have the victory. Each prophet of God is filled with purpose from the day that we were conceived in our mother's womb. God has a plan. He has called each of us to walk out in its entirety for His glory. This is your prophetic destiny. The road will not always be easy. The burden will not always be light. There will be struggles, doubt, temptation, fear, haters, and more. This is life and we will be tested. Again, I tell you to adopt the mindset to defeat the obstacles in your life and achieve in God.

With God, all things are possible. We are to be confident in that prophet. When you have discovered your purpose and begun to walk in it, be prepared for the attack of the enemy. This is why some of you are under the attacks you are dealing with now! Be strong!

4. Always give commands to satan and his demons in Jesus' name. Those prophets who will really, truly believe and stay in the presence of God have been given the authority to cast out demons. Prophets, we are to break the power of the demonic tongue and we are to cast down imaginations in our own lives as well as in others.

Words have power and each time they are spoken, they convince the receiver it's the truth. Who is the source of your words? We can't afford any more satanic brainwashing, especially when the Words are not the Word of God.

Prophet, are you the exponent speaking the Word of God or are you speaking death to yourself and everybody you are connected to? So we must be able to cast down demonic words and rebuke them in the name of Jesus.

As a prophet, you have the authority to rebuke them. Satan has to go, no matter how far away someone may be, or how hopeless the situation may look. "Satan doesn't have any power over you; the only thing he has is the ability to deceive." *Proverbs 18:21* says, *"Death and life are in the power of the tongue."*

Prophets, according to *2 Corinthians 10:5,* you also have the authority to cast down those imaginations as they dare exalt themselves against the knowledge of God.

5. Always submit yourself to God in the presence of satan. The Bible tells us that in *James 4:7,* we are to *"submit ourselves to God."* We then resist the devil and look for him to go away from us. This is the Word of God. He will flee. *Zechariah 3:2* clearly tells us that it is the Lord who rebukes satan and not us. That is important as even in our work for God. We need to know and understand what we are to do.

Our focus is and should be on our work for Christ. We are to follow Christ. He is able to defeat the forces of evil. Prophet, you have the full armor to stand with you against evil. Your faith, wisdom, and knowledge about God and His Word are your tools. This is a sticking point as prophets are developed. We see them skipping wisdom and knowledge and they wonder why faith never develops.

6. Always stop satan from communicating with his demons. Demonic transmissions are real and they are working daily. Demonic transmissions are the Luciferian's communication cycle with his imps. Just like we are in the Army of the Lord, satan too has his own little army.

Satan has hordes of helpers. We have discussed several of them in this book and our primary reference has been on his manifestation of the Luciferian spirit. What you need to understand is that demonic imps are dumb. They do not think for themselves. They follow orders and they do it well. They work on detailed assignments to which they are highly dedicated.

Prophets, realize that any army without effective communication will be defeated. The devil attempts to block our communications with the Holy Ghost headquarters by way of spiritual attacks through mental captivation.

When a prophet's mind is captivated, it has been charmed by seducing spirits and kidnapped. Ultimately, the attention of that person is rerouted. This is what will kill and destroy a prophet. This is the influence within the prophetic of the Luciferian spirit. This is why we see prophets so many times disrespectful, unroyal, and undisciplined.

They are dealing with what is called captivation or the hijacking of the mind in a deceptive manner. Because the mind can send transmissions to the body to tell it what to do, we see the target of the enemy. The enemy infiltrates and has a goal to contaminate and destroy.

Make no mistake, the stream of demonic transmissions must be broken. So, how does the devil communicate with a prophet?

1. The ideas, thoughts, and imagination of a prophet.
2. The enemies' finesse. The select words and voice pitch!
3. Demonic transmission vehicles: a person, place, or thing.
4. Getting attention and not knowing how to handle it.
5. Makes you think that everyone is against you.

So Prophet, know that you must stop this. Prophetic liberation from demonic transmissions and the enemy's communication tactics is developing the ability to employ the command of our mind through and by the power of God. We must recognize thoughts that are not of God. We must not submit to the ministry of torment. We must identify these thoughts and send them back immediately.

Prophet, there is a difference between your mind and your thoughts. Look at it like this as your mind is the vehicle. Prophet, your thoughts are what allows you to get into your vehicle and ride. We need to know what to pick up and what not to pick up.

The enemy wants your mind, and the reality is that your soul that will be his battlefield. He will continue with his drama. This is who he is. You and I must be who we are. Always remember that the Luciferian spirit desires your soul. This is why we must have the mind of Christ. It is a safeguard against mental terrorism. Prophetic mentality is essential.

7. Always speak peace, love, and power to yourself. *Proverbs 18:20-21* says, *"Your belly will be satisfied with the fruit of your mouth as we see that death and life are in the power of our tongues."* Prophets go through some things in life that are unnecessary and it's because of what comes out of their mouths.

Prophet, your mouth will feed you or your mouth can curse you. Some of us are in bad situations or hard times because of what we say or have said. Your life will follow what you say. You are the director of the occurrences in your life and in the name of Jesus.

Your mouth carries the deposit of wealth, prosperity, death, or negativity into your life or someone else's life. Prophet, learn how to speak life into your situation and encourage yourself when the enemy attacks.

Call on the name of God and reassure yourself and your situation. You don't have to accept anything less than what God has for you. Prophet, fill your mind and feel the peace of God that passes all understanding. You will stand still and see the salvation of the Lord.

8. Always break the assignment or stronghold that satan has established concerning the attack. Strongholds examples are "demon possession," a grip, persistent oppression, obsessions, hindrances, or harassment. Many prophets are the victims of satan's strongholds.

The devil's strategy is to disguise his activities. He wants them to appear that someone or something else is to blame. This is why the Luciferian spirit is so effective. He wants us to get our attention on his surrogates instead of the "real source." He is the real source, I say again.

9. Stop all the motions or actions of the devil and control your thinking. Prophet, your life is always asking you to make this one choice. Your negative thinking is nothing but resistance to life itself. Change your mind and you will change your life.

Come against the ministry of torment via the Luciferian spirit. Bring light to expose the negative thought patterns of your life and others. Then you will realize there was no truth to them to start with. Prophets do not fall for the ministry of torment; it is of the devil.

10. Always render the demons inactive. The description of the demon-possessed man is in *Luke 8.* He is located in the country of the Gadarenes. He lives among tombs and he is totally tormented by satan.

Think about how he now sees Jesus from afar. He ran and worshiped Him. He is crying out and asking for help. His actions speak louder than His words here. He says, "What have I to do with You, Jesus, Son of the Highest God? I implore You by God that You do not torment me." For He said to him, "Come out of the man, unclean spirit!" This is a classic profile of demonic possession.

The ancient superstition of spiritual power over another if you knew or said their full exact name was in effect. The Luciferian spirit and his imps knew Jesus. Jesus was addressed with his full title, which did not work for them. Prophets, always listen to how people address you. It will speak volumes about who they are.

Demonic possession is a still a reality today. Prophets, we must guard against either ignoring demonic activity or over-emphasizing supposed demonic activity. This is really real. The demons want to inhabit our bodies for the same reason a violent man wants a gun. They both need weapons.

The Luciferian spirit hates the image of God in you. They want to make you grotesque. Remember the man in the country of the Gadarenes. Demonic spirits can both deceive and intimidate Prophets, binding them with fear and unbelief.

Prophets, let's be clear. Our fight continues, but we are up for the challenge. God is on our side. We must be up for the challenge, as this spirit still lurks today among apostles and prophets. The Luciferian Spirit is still here to destroy.

CHAPTER 12

THE LUCIFERIAN SPIRIT IS STILL HERE TO DESTROY

The effect of the Luciferian spirit on the destiny of apostles and prophets today is birthed in perspectives and interpretations. There is no doubt that the Luciferian spirit affects the destiny of apostles and prophets, and it is very complex.

The concept of the Luciferian spirit affecting the beliefs of the apostles and prophets is evident. We must look at our perspectives on the roles of apostles and prophets. This will vary by our cultures for sure. The foundational gifts today will vary as they offer perspective on the Luciferian spirit and its effect on apostles and prophets as they move to understand and seek their destiny.

Just as the church of today is bound with complexity, theological drama from different faiths to different theological interpretations and spiritual beliefs, the topic of the Luciferian spirit will be different. The world today asks us to respect and show sensitivity to diverse religious perspectives. Prophets, let's be clear. We need to be careful not to lose our focus. There is clearly so much blocking us today, but I submit the issue starts with us.

Let me submit the game the Luciferian spirit plays with us. Think and consider the following. Have you ever felt that maybe you have been a barrier or a block to your destiny? Yes, you are an apostle, prophet, and foundation gift of the church. This is according to *Ephesians 2:20.* The cornerstone gifts of the church are so often the most scrutinized and the most attacked.

I have shared with you various individual areas where the Luciferian spirit has worked and worked well, now allow me to share from the foundational gift perspective.

How many groups of believers do we see who are intent on not in-cluding these two gifts of the 5-fold ministry within their fellowship? Some would rather block out the apostle and the prophet for various reasons. Have you ever wondered why people act the way they do towards prophets and apostles?

Consider the fact that some have been hurt and not been educated in the 5-fold ministry concept of *Ephesians chapter 4.* The gifts of the apostle and prophet were not considered as relevant in the church or ministry they grew up in. Then there is the fact that some simply do not believe in the concept of a 5-fold ministry.

All that is true and continues to be an issue but what about the apostle and what about the prophet who need to understand but do not understand their personal process of destiny?

Over and over, we see this apostle or prophet and they are in love with tomorrow and not today. They are in love with who they want to be tomorrow and fail to address the issues of their lives today. This is the point of the Luciferian spirit attack. The spirit attacks and imparts the need for prophets and apostles to arrive today because tomorrow is begging for them.

For those of you who have read this book, the focus has been on the method of identifying the Luciferian spirit. The key issue is how fast we see the loss of focus on today's apostles and prophets. So often we lack the ability to realize that today is important because without today, tomorrow does not matter. Reaching your destiny is learning how to master your current step on the way to your next step in life. Here is where the Luciferian spirit wants you to skip today and jump to tomorrow.

The Luciferian spirit will have you searching for validation, and a place in the body of Christ, and they never seem to grow. Apostles and prophets so often, do not realize that in the struggle to understand and grow, they could very well be their biggest obstacle to fulfilling their God-given destiny. I say they because the Luciferian spirit works in the dark.

This in-the-dark master worker holds a prophet or apostle back from building fruitful and anointed relationships. What issues of life are before us that hold us in a place of stalemate? Let's look at our mentality.

1 Corinthians 13:11 says, *"When I was a child, the word of God says that I thought, talked, and acted as a child. When I became a man/woman, the word says that childish things were put away."* This is so important because we look at the world in a certain way. Could it be that the Luciferian spirit wants to keep us immature children?

Let's look closely at the two different communication systems. The two systems need to be addressed in the life of the work of the apostle or prophet. There is the system of the child or immature mentality and the system of being a mature adult. Let me be clear. The

Luciferian spirit wants to keep you as a spoiled child and not a mature functioning gift of God.

We need to examine each to understand the effect each has. This will affect the life of an apostle or prophet as far as development. This is directly affected by how we see our destiny. The destiny of an apostle or prophet will never be understood or reached until they change their communication from a child to an adult. Unless we break the spell of the Luciferian spirit, we will always be as a spoiled child.

Thinking, speaking, and understanding as a child differs from thinking, speaking, and understanding as an adult. Let's consider how we look at others and how we look at ourselves. We will always test others by how they think, speak, and what they do or do not understand. The Luciferian spirit does not want you to think and function in a mature manner.

As apostles and prophets, do we have the personal courage to test the fact that we may be operating as kids or children when our position requires us to operate as adults? What are we communicating or holding on to that limits us in our assignments and clouds our destiny? We must be willing to identify it and deal with it, even if it means ourselves.

This is the key to understanding our destiny. Do we function at the level we need to function and more importantly, are we aware we need to test ourselves? This is a fair question we need to ask ourselves!

How many of us know and understand that many of us in the prophetic and apostolic gifts are loyal to our own dysfunctions? Has the Luciferian spirit got us wrapped up in a mode of being stubborn to hold on to ways that clearly are not working? We must answer this question for ourselves before we seek to help others.

We claim growth, but it is not leading you to your destiny because you may be thinking, acting, or even communicating as a child. How many of us have heard phrases such as "That's how I am, or speak for yourself"? We all have heard "this is the way God told me to do it."

Why do we not consider the fact that the way, we say we are is not working? A better question is, how much longer will so many of us hold on to our dysfunctions and allow life to simply pass us by? What would happen if we would understand or look at this from another perspective? The key here is the activity of the demonic force at work. This is what keeps us immature kids.

We are doing things as a child in an environment that we need to do as adults. We are hurting ourselves. Today, we see the differences between prophets and apostles even within their ranks. The childish ways have separated us greatly within the ranks of the apostolic and Prophetic. The core issue that separates them is how they communicate. Once again, this is what the Luciferian spirit does.

This is how they speak, think, and act. Can you see that the way you think, speak and act is the announcement of your maturity or you being immature or childish? This is the link to your destiny. Stop right here and focus on how you are dealing with this in your life right now, today.

It is hard to understand that God is putting you in positions of influence and because of how you see them and feel about them, you do not understand your journey to your destiny. The journey to your destiny starts by dealing with the issues in front of you today. We see the Luciferian spirit effect as we see no need to grow today; we just want to go forth.

This is so critical to the prophet and apostle as we relate to the Body of Christ. The real issue is the inability to understand the need for change in an apostle or prophet. This is the status of the inner man within each of us. Do we search ourselves daily or just want to go forth and any cost?

What am I saying? The outer life of the apostle and the prophet are seen and they are fine. The outer life matures, but the real issue is that we are children, internally and we demonstrate it with immaturity. I submit once again, that the Luciferian spirit keeps us this way.

David was king and he was still acting like a child on the inside. He was acting like a child to get what he wanted and what he knew was not his. We all know about his situation with Uriah's wife. He was mature but his actions were childish and selfish. This is a real concept that holds much truth.

David becomes a modern-day metaphor for us to demonstrate that we, in a lot of ways, are still children. We are grown on the outside but a kid on the inside. We look at our lives as children. Are we, as apostles and prophets, ignoring our childish ways while we are still trying to lead others?

What is the answer? Look again at *1 Corinthians 13:11*. There is a keyword "but." You can put away your childish ways but that will not make you a man or a woman. Again David was a full-grown man and still was a child on the inside. Can you see the inside work of the Luciferian spirit? This is the demonstrated effect we witness in prophetic circles, especially when authority is granted sooner than the maturity mandates.

Throughout the body of Christ, we have apostles and prophets who are fully grown and yet still demonstrate childish behavior. They are of age. They are in positions of authority, and yet the influence they have is that of a child. They have not put away their childish ways.

There is no understanding of what it means. That is a choice that they have not exercised because of a lack of understanding of the power of changing a mentality. This is clearly what the Luciferian spirit hopes you never find out.

Can you understand that many of us in the apostolic and prophetic are still childish on the inside? Yes, we all, in one way or another, are dealing with the Luciferian spirit. Think about it. We have actually outgrown the way we communicate, think, and act. We have only done this on the outside, but not on the inside. This is where we need to make the changes.

How many of us will admit that we have outgrown the way we act sometimes? We speak one thing and we actually mean something altogether different. Do we realize that we need to put some things away? What are we loyal to? This type of confusion in our lives is reflective of the spell of the Luciferian spirit and we don't seem to realize it.

We are to put some things away in our lives like our childish actions. They are systematically killing us and destroying our relationships with each other. Our growth as foundation pieces of the gospel will never be realized until we understand that it works both ways.

Our functionality to respond as a child is diminished when we take charge and put some things out of our lives. Our childish ways restrict us from operating in the Glory of God.

Look at Apostle Paul and how he moved from his selfish ways and quickly matured into a leader of inspiration and revelation. Paul had what many of us did not have, and that was a Damascus moment. Read *Acts 9* about how the unholy alliance was broken off his life.

Apostle Paul is clear and direct when he says to put them away. He is talking about our ways. The childish ways that restrict us from reaching our destiny must be let go of.

Simply look at Paul's life, and you will see that he put his childish ways away. Look at everything he let go of in his life. Leaders think of the prophets who need to learn this important concept. Remember, the prophets who were under this Luciferian influence and never realized it. Remember this list can include you and me.

Paul teaches us that we must identify what is childish in our lives. Unless we identify it each and every time, we will carry weight and issues that have nothing to do with our progress. This is the essence of the Luciferian spirit and the effect it seeks to have on the apostles and prophets of today.

What I am saying is that we must put away what we have been defending with our actions for so long. Truth be told, far too many of us have refused and if we will look around in the Body of Christ and the prophetic community, we are not as one, but we can get there. We must do the needed work, not on each other, but within ourselves. I so strongly feel this is why the Luciferian spirit goes undetected and camouflages itself to stay undetected and unnoticed.

There has been out and out competition within the prophetic and if you have been around it for more than a day or two, you should have witnessed it. My focus is not gloom and doom. My focus is to elevate this gift. We must however start with us and stop pointing at each other and using social media to preach and teach on what everyone is doing wrong to include your leadership. Do I need to welcome the Luciferian spirit, or have we done a good job of that already?

Understanding will heal a multitude of issues. The term understanding is what we refer to as the truth that we stand on and under. The power of understanding is what will separate us from being a child to being an adult. This is how and why we must move forward from where we are at and not skip today for tomorrow.

The mentality of a mature prophet or a mature apostle is all about understanding. This will render the Luciferian spirit useless and powerless. What we choose to understand or not understand is killing us as apostles or prophets.

When the apostles and prophets of this now generation learn how to pull themselves from where they started then and only then will we make a difference in the lives of those to whom they are sent to by God. Let's work together as God works through us to defeat the Luciferian spirit.

ABOUT THE AUTHOR

Apostle Ken Cox started serving God in 1994 after a series of unforeseen life failures. Out of the military and seemly starting life over again, by 2000, Apostle Cox had found his life calling as a Prophet.

The challenge of learning and understanding presented a new frontier. Apostle Cox dove into the process and has now emerged as a well traveled prophet who serves the Body of Christ as an Apostle.

Apostle Cox, along with his wife, Prophetess Sabina Cox are the leaders of Where Eagles Fly Fellowship Inc., a fellowship of prophets and apostle across the USA and beyond who are dedicated and focused on establishing the prophetic gift back into society as they raise up prophets around the country and abroad.

Apostle Cox and Prophetess Cox are available for Revivals, Conferences and Meetings. They have been featured in meetings and sought-after to teach and instruct the prophetic for ministries seeking to learn more about the gift. Apostle and Prophetess Cox have 3 children and 4 grandkids as of this writing and currently reside in Durham, NC. Contact them through the Where Eagles Fly office at 919-695-3375 or 919-213-1328 or at www.whereeaglesfly.us.

INDEX

A

Aaron, 8
Abraham, 25, 26, 28, 29, 30, 33, 43
Absalom, 12, 31, 81
Absalom spirit, 12
accidents, 102, 103, 105
adults, 115, 116
adversary, 1, 7, 44
agenda, 4, 31, 78
Ahab, 31
alcoholism, 64
allegiance, 13
ambition, 3, 78
Ancestors, 66
angel, 3, 44, 45
animal, 44
anointed, 31, 34, 40, 66, 88, 114
anointing, 12, 26, 38, 74, 90, 91, 92, 93, 94, 95, 97, 100
Apostle Ken Cox, 121
Apostle Paul, 8, 78, 118, 119
Apostles, 5, 6, 13, 20, 101, 114
army, 107, 108
arrogant, 11, 15, 16

assignments, 68, 107, 115
audience, 28

B

Babylon, 58, 60
Babylonian exile, 57
Balaam, 34, 35, 36, 37, 38, 39, 40, 41, 42, 43, 44, 45, 46, 47, 53, 54, 55
Balak, 36, 38, 40
bathroom, 25, 31
battlefield, 49, 109
behavior, 13, 67, 68, 78, 117
believers, 78, 113
betrayal, 12
blessings, 86, 90, 97, 100
Body of Christ, 19, 52, 79, 80, 84, 117, 119, 121
breach, 70, 71, 79
business, 75

C

camouflage, 34
cancer, 66
celebrate, 56
challenge, 20, 29, 53, 57, 66, 111, 121
chaos, 11
character, 16, 21, 29, 53, 100, 101
charisma, 73
child abuse, 87
children, 36, 69, 114, 115, 117, 121
Christians, 80
church, 21, 65, 74, 80, 88, 89, 90, 93, 112, 113

churches, 32, 52, 56, 66, 80, 81

civilizations, 77

cloud, 96

comfort zone, 29

common sense, 84

communication, 12, 27, 57, 70, 82, 103, 104, 107, 108, 114, 115

community, 27, 61, 101

company, 30, 94

competition, 52, 61, 75, 119

conflict, 30, 52, 76

confusion, 11, 32, 52, 105, 118

congregation, 6

conviction, 41

Conviction, 39

correction, 15

corruption, 50

cots, 94

counterfeit, 92

countries, 16

country, 7, 90, 110, 111, 121

covenant partners, 25

crisis, 49

Crowds, 95

Cultural trends, 34

cultures, 16, 72, 79, 112

curses, 12, 62, 63, 64, 65, 66, 67, 68, 69, 71, 88

D

Daniel, 59, 85

dark realm, 46

darkness, 13, 47

Darkness, 46

David, 117

death, 15, 64, 106, 109

debate, 27, 45, 93

deception, 3, 50, 83

Deception, 1

Deliverance, 66

demeanor, 16, 20

demonic attack, 23

demonic entities, 1

demonic tongue, 106

demon-possessed man, 110

demons, 65, 103, 106, 107, 110, 111

depression, 53, 59, 64

descendants, 13, 64

destiny, 16, 32, 106, 112, 113, 114, 115, 116, 119

destroy, 1, 2, 19, 22, 24, 40, 47, 67, 76, 87, 93, 101, 108, 111, 112

destruction, 5, 11, 23, 25, 47, 57, 72

Devil, 4

diabetes, 66

diamond, 100

directives, 10, 29, 30

disappointment, 52

discernment, 9, 16, 18

disciples, 6, 98

disobedience, 27, 45

division, 51, 52

domestic violence, 87

donkey, 42, 44, 45

door, 19, 35, 56

doubt, 19, 23, 43, 52, 54, 70, 77, 88, 94, 106, 112

drama, 70, 109, 112

drug abuse, 87

dysfunctions, 115, 116

E

earthly riches, 39
education, 12
ego, 14, 99
elevation, 15, 19
Elijah, 50
Elisha, 12, 13
embarrass, 22, 44, 73
emotions, 46, 72
empower, 51, 52, 56, 61, 80
enemy, 1, 14, 26, 51, 56, 67, 68, 80, 86, 101, 106, 108, 109
evil presence, 65
evil spirit, 18, 64, 65
eyes, 8, 44, 64
Ezekiel, 56, 57, 58, 59, 60

F

failure, 5, 100
faith, 19, 63, 93, 95, 98, 99, 107
false gods, 50
false prophet, 35
family, 12, 13, 15, 18, 28, 30, 32, 64, 97
family lineage, 15
faults, 12, 94, 99
favor, 1, 46, 78, 84, 100
fears, 54
fees of divination, 38, 41
fellowship, 58, 59, 74, 83, 113, 121
fellowships, 56
financial affairs, 19

financial covenants, 19, 20

fire, 96

fool, 5, 82

foundation, 25, 72, 113, 118

freedom, 76, 83

friend, 1, 7, 25, 32, 57, 73, 75, 89

friends, 9, 57, 76, 90, 97

fruits of righteousness, 8

frustration, 52, 79, 80

G

Garden of Eden, 43

garments, 102

Gehazi, 12, 13, 14, 15, 19

generation, 4, 34, 50, 51, 54, 56, 60, 63, 64, 66, 67, 68, 71, 72, 78, 88, 120

generational roots, 62

genes, 64

get-rich schemes, 67

Glory, 90, 96, 118

goal, 2, 3, 84, 85, 90, 108

God, 1, 2, 3, 4, 5, 6, 7, 8, 12, 15, 19, 20, 21, 22, 24, 25, 26, 27, 28, 29, 30, 31, 32, 33, 34, 35, 36, 37, 38, 39, 40, 41, 42, 43, 44, 45, 46, 47, 48, 49, 50, 52, 53, 54, 55, 56, 57, 58, 59, 60, 63, 66, 67, 68, 69, 72, 74, 75, 76, 78, 79, 80, 83, 84, 85, 86, 88, 89, 90, 91, 92, 93, 94, 95, 96, 97, 98, 99, 100, 101, 102, 103, 104, 105, 106, 107, 108, 109, 110, 111, 114, 115, 116, 118, 120, 121

Gomorrah, 30

gospel, 94, 118

gossip, 29, 32, 50, 75, 87

greatness, 30, 49

greed, 13, 51

grumble, 19
guilt, 54

H

Haggai, 57
harassment, 110
haters, 89, 106
hazards, 103
healing, 92, 93, 99
health problems, 64
heart, 3, 39, 41, 42, 54, 67, 68, 69, 98
heaven, 3
herdsmen, 30
history, 37, 76, 77, 84, 93, 102
Holy Ghost, 99, 108
Holy Spirit, 95, 96
honor, 7, 8, 15, 18, 32, 33, 40, 48, 51, 69, 72, 89, 103
human nature, 56
humanity, 77, 84
humility, 11, 48, 100
hungry, 14, 19, 54, 89

I

Immature prophets, 75
imps, 51, 107, 111
influence, 7, 18, 19, 27, 31, 34, 38, 46, 51, 55, 59, 63, 67, 68, 69, 77, 78, 88, 90, 104, 108, 116, 118, 119
insecurities, 54
Isaiah, 3, 4, 5, 59
Israel, 34, 36

J

jealous, 73, 87
jealousy, 50, 53
Jeremiah, 56, 57, 58, 59, 60, 71, 72
Jerusalem, 59, 71, 94
Jesus, 6, 7, 50, 64, 68, 71, 90, 93, 97, 98, 99, 101, 104, 105, 106, 109, 110, 111
Jezebel, 1, 31
Jezebel Spirit, 1
job, 42, 57, 66, 77, 103, 120
John, 93, 94
Judah, 57, 60
judgmental, 8, 74
justice, 60

K

kids, 90, 115, 116
King of Babylon, 3, 4
kingdom, 2, 20, 39, 40, 48, 99, 101, 103
kings, 85
knowledge, 4, 8, 9, 20, 69, 76, 77, 83, 84, 85, 107

L

labor, 18
leaders, 4, 5, 6, 8, 11, 13, 14, 15, 16, 18, 19, 20, 21, 22, 23, 30, 38, 40, 42, 44, 50, 51, 52, 54, 66, 70, 71, 79, 81, 83, 84, 85, 88, 104, 121
leadership, 5, 7, 10, 12, 15, 19, 22, 30, 31, 48, 52, 61, 81, 83, 86, 87, 120
learning phase, 11
leprosy, 13

lethal, 20

lies, 11, 53

lone ranger prophet, 89

love, 8, 9, 15, 16, 18, 27, 43, 48, 56, 61, 73, 74, 78, 79, 88, 109, 113

Lucifer, 1, 3, 4, 6, 7, 35, 47, 92

Luciferian spirit, 1, 2, 4, 6, 7, 8, 11, 12, 13, 14, 15, 18, 19, 20, 21, 22, 23, 24, 26, 27, 28, 29, 31, 33, 34, 35, 37, 40, 41, 43, 44, 45, 46, 47, 48, 49, 50, 51, 52, 53, 55, 56, 57, 58, 59, 60, 61, 62, 63, 64, 65, 66, 67, 68, 69, 70, 71, 72, 76, 77, 78, 79, 80, 81, 82, 83, 84, 85, 86, 89, 90, 91, 92, 93, 96, 97, 98, 99, 101, 102, 103, 104, 105, 107, 108, 109, 110, 111, 112, 113, 114, 115, 116, 117, 118, 119, 120

Luciferian system, 6

M

manifestation, 4, 24, 26, 28, 31, 32, 33, 47, 104, 107

mantle, 31, 35, 37, 88

marriage, 33

master, 1, 6, 48, 51, 80, 114

maturity, 10, 21, 35, 52, 116, 117

mediums, 47

melody, 49

mental illness, 66

mentality, 47, 49, 79, 109, 114, 118, 120

mentor, 28, 61

mentorship, 22, 97, 98

messages, 34, 77, 84

Midian, 35

mindfulness, 54

ministries, 50, 52, 58, 59, 66, 78, 87, 121

ministry, 11, 15, 22, 23, 28, 30, 32, 35, 53, 55, 59, 65, 66, 70, 72, 73, 74, 75, 79, 80, 87, 88, 90, 93, 101, 108, 110, 113

ministry circles, 15

Miriam, 8
Moab, 36, 38, 42, 44
money, 19, 41, 52, 75
morning star, 7
Moses, 8
mouthpiece, 103, 105

N

Naaman, 12
nationalities, 16
nationality, 86
Nations, 26
negative energy, 55, 63
nephew, 25, 33
new age, 80
New Testament, 50, 99
notoriety, 5, 10, 35
novice, 37
now-generation prophets, 4, 51, 72, 88

O

obstacles, 106
occult powers, 66
offended, 72, 88
Old Testament, 50, 79, 92
opposition, 50
oppression, 72, 110
ordained, 20, 22, 98

P

pallets, 94

passion, 48, 49, 50, 68, 74

pastors, 20

peace, 7, 18, 32, 83, 109

peers, 11, 15, 21, 49, 53, 59, 73, 85, 88, 89

perception, 8, 37

Peter, 92, 93, 94, 95, 96, 97, 98, 99, 100, 101

power, 34, 50, 51, 64, 67, 69, 77, 84, 92, 93, 94, 96, 104, 106, 108, 109, 111, 118, 120

pray, 8, 32, 55, 66, 69, 100, 103, 104

prayer, 13, 16, 31, 53, 66, 96, 100, 103

pride, 3, 14, 23, 50, 80, 87

profession, 102

prophesy, 20, 31, 58, 65

Prophet, 1, 2, 4, 6, 7, 18, 19, 21, 22, 23, 24, 25, 26, 27, 28, 29, 30, 31, 32, 33, 34, 35, 36, 37, 38, 39, 41, 43, 47, 49, 55, 56, 57, 60, 64, 67, 68, 69, 71, 72, 75, 79, 80, 81, 82, 86, 95, 96, 100, 102, 104, 105, 106, 107, 108, 109, 110, 121

Prophet Lot, 22, 23, 24, 25, 26, 27, 28, 29, 30, 31, 32, 33

prophetess, 16

Prophetess Sabina Cox, 121

prophetic breaches, 69, 71, 72, 76, 77, 79, 80, 81

prophetic community, 2, 4, 7, 51, 57, 58, 72, 78, 88, 99, 104, 119

prophetic conference, 25

prophetic daughter, 5

prophetic group, 10, 14, 21, 45, 61, 65

prophetic insights, 77

prophetic lessons, 21

prophetic level, 87

prophetic meetings, 24, 54

prophetic office, 16

prophetic overseer, 70

prophetic ranks, 49, 59, 76

prophetic realm, 2, 4, 57
prophetic son, 5, 15, 23, 54
prophetic taxis, 14, 21
prophetic words, 71, 79
prosperity, 20, 55, 68, 100, 109
protocol, 21, 32, 57

R

racism, 50
rebellion, 3, 50, 81, 83
Redeemer, 98
regrets, 54
relationship, 19, 23, 27, 36, 39, 43, 53, 56, 57, 71, 73, 94, 97
religious institutions, 52
religious teachings, 51
repent, 46
reputation, 37, 81
resentment, 76
restaurant, 25
revelation, 12, 77, 84, 86, 95, 118
Revivals, 121
reward, 54, 100
rivalry, 47, 48, 49, 50, 52, 53, 55, 56, 58, 59, 60
roaming prophet, 82, 87, 89
rose, 93

S

saints, 32
Satan, 1, 3, 46, 47, 64, 103, 104, 106, 107
school of the prophets, 25
season, 4, 53, 90

Second Temple, 57

secret agent, 28

security, 18

seed, 12, 14, 104

seer, 16, 28, 53, 93

self-development, 17

self-elevate, 11

self-esteem, 60

self-examination, 86

self-gratification, 99

self-reflection, 53, 83

self-righteous, 7, 8

senior prophet, 10, 11, 40

senior prophets, 2, 5, 6, 13, 19, 52

servant, 6, 12, 95, 104

sex abuse, 87

sexism, 50

shame, 16, 53, 54

Shem, 34

Shunammite woman, 12

shy, 16, 46, 53

sibling, 76

sick, 92, 93, 94, 95, 97

sinful decisions, 26

sinners, 49, 86

sister prophets, 61

slavery, 59

smear campaigns, 28

sneaky, 46

social media, 29, 51, 57, 70, 77, 119

society, 34, 46, 50, 51, 57, 84, 121

Sodom, 25, 30

soul, 4, 32, 40, 41, 48, 49, 50, 109

special gifts, 5

spectrum, 12, 28, 52, 61, 70

spirits, 1, 7, 8, 46, 47, 51, 56, 64, 65, 92, 94, 95, 108, 111

spiritual beliefs, 112

spiritual bondage, 63

states, 16

strangers, 65

strife, 14

student, 4, 6, 98, 103

suicide, 103

symbols, 34

T

teach, 5, 119, 121

teacher, 6, 98

temptation, 47, 54, 80, 106

terrorism, 109

The Shadow Anointing, 91, 92

throne, 3, 6, 20

tradition, 27

training, 12, 20, 21, 22, 52, 84

Trauma, 105

troublesome issues, 55

trust, 23, 28, 30, 52, 61, 76, 78, 95, 101

truth, 43, 50, 54, 61, 105, 106, 110, 117, 120

U

unbelief, 12, 19, 111

ungodly counsel, 87, 89

upsetting, 71

V

validation, 84, 114
victim, 2, 13, 23, 87
victims, 15, 110
victory, 103, 105
vision, 26, 33, 87, 88
voice, 19, 24, 35, 37, 108

W

war, 47, 49, 50, 51, 52, 53, 54, 56, 64, 75
Where Eagles Fly Fellowship Inc, 121
whisper, 29
wife, 25, 90, 117, 121
wisdom, 12, 13, 20, 72, 83, 84, 85, 86, 87, 88, 89, 90, 107
Witchcraft, 66
witness, 27, 117
world, 3, 15, 26, 27, 68, 86, 94, 102, 112, 114
writer, 78

Z

zeal, 15, 27, 52
Zechariah, 57, 107

www.ingramcontent.com/pod-product-compliance
Lightning Source LLC
Chambersburg PA
CBHW071005120626
46546CB00003B/945